Geometry of the Golden Section

Robert VINCENT

Translated from French by Adrienne MEQUIN

CHALAGAM PUBLISHING

Artistic creation, design,
illustrations, photos, first cover
(from a drawing by MARC THÉRON):
ROBERT CHALAVOUX

First French Edition, June 1999 by CHALAGAM
Tittle "Géométrie du nombre d'or"

by ROBERT VINCENT (Public works Engineer, Paris)
ISBN 2-950 80001-2-2

Second English edition March 2007
ISBN 2-951 9607-3-5
(It is the translation by ADRIENNE MEQUIN of the 5rd edition
of "Géométrie du nombre d'or" by ROBERT VINCENT
Chalagam Édition, ISBN 2-951 9607-2-7 March 2007).

Printed by SVI,Mauguio, France website: www.svi-publicep.fr

Chalagam Edition — 15, boulevard André-Aune, 13006 Marseille, France
Siret 384 159 018 00017 - Code APE 221 A

Télephone 33 (0)4 91 55 66 77 — Fax 33 (0)4 91 55 66 21
e-mail: edition@chalagam.com
website: http//www.chalagam.com

Distributed by CHALAGAM

contents

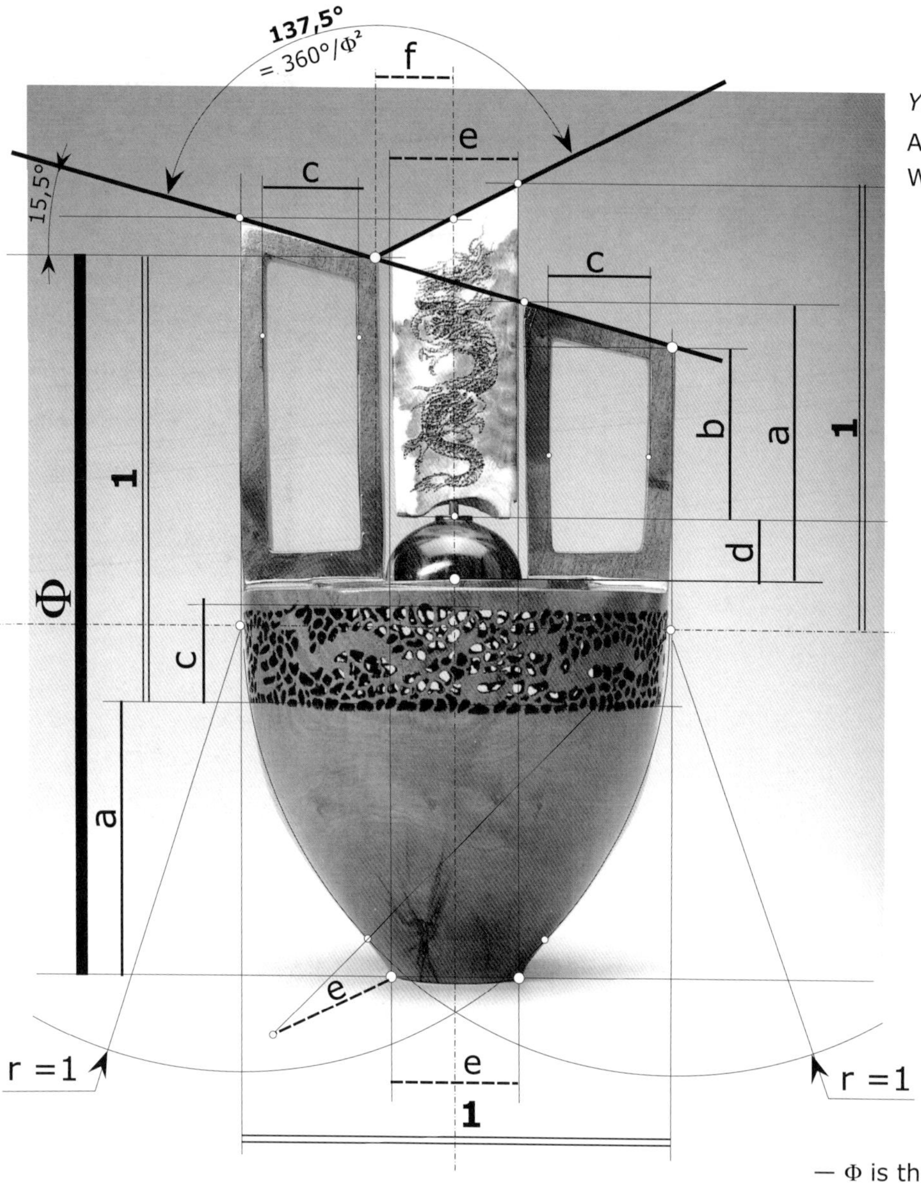

Year of the Dragon

A piece by **Binh Pho**

Woodturner, Illinois, USA.

Binh Pho has not taken into account the golden section. This experienced artist has created a piece in which the ratios of the dimensions are very close to a theoretical design represented here according to the dimensions calculated. He has found the right proportions instinctively because in his own words: "it looks good".

$a = 1 / \Phi$

$b = 1 / \Phi^2$

$c = 1 / \Phi^3$

$d = 1 / \Phi^4$

$e = c \times \sqrt{\Phi}$

$f = d \times \sqrt{\Phi}$

— Φ is the golden number = 1.618...

— 137.5° is the "angle of Fibonacci", that can be met in "phyllotaxie" (study of the layout of branches around the trunk or of leaves on the stem).

Publisher's note:

Albert LeCoff represents an association of artists looking for beauty and accomplishing works themselves guided by their sensitivity, supported by their knowledge and their experience.
This is why we have chosen him to write the preface of this book and also because we can consider him to represent the lovers of wood-turning, cabinet-making, or patch-work and all the creators of works of art.

We want to show a permanence in art, since the artists of the pharaonic dynasty down to the contemporary ones , passing by the Middle Ages cathedral builders. Their designs are all rigourously the same whether they are made with creepers, knotted ropes, compass and rulers or thanks to computers! The figures proposed here fulfill the desire of those who love old stones as well as of the avant garde creators in all fields.

preface

Albert LeCoff

Executive Director of the Wood Turning Center,
Philadelphia, PA, USA*

The publisher has done me the honor of asking me to write the preface. He has chosen to illustrate it with Binh Pho's work of art.

This is the publisher's aim :
"We want to show a permanence in art, from the artists of the pharaonic dynasty down to the contemporary ones, passing by the Middle Ages cathedral builders. Their designs are all rigourously the same..."

In this preface I would like to develop the following idea : in art, geometry is universal and timeless!

In Euclid's time (1st century B.C), a lot of mathematical problems were solved by geometry. This is no longer possible today because of the complexity and precision required to reach, for example, a precise point in the eye with a laser beam.

From time immemorial, artists have created works destined to be admired; precision was not necessary. Building geometric figures is very useful to solve the artists' problems, proportion being often the main difficulty.

Thanks to Robert Vincent's book we can discover, from Antiquity down to present days, that proportion requires the "mean and extreme ratio" known as the "Golden Section", the "Golden Number" or the "Modulor".

Those are the different names given to that unique proportion, according to the period, to the artists and their achievements.
The ratio, now called "Phi", is worth 1.618...
Phi is a number, the "Golden Number", and the proportion that brings it into existence is commonly called the "Golden Section".

Why define it as "Gold", "Golden", "Divine"? Because that number undeniably exists in Nature: for example in the very heart of a simple thistle, in seashells, in flowers, and trees.

Phi is a "jewel" comparable to gold. Moreover, it is within ourselves-which made it "divine" in the eyes of Pacioli, a 15th century monk.

The ancient measurements were based on the body (inch, foot, cubit...) in the phi ratio. It is a "natural" proportion. That is probably why it seems harmonious to man.

It is normal for experienced artists to have an accurate eye for that proportion and to respect it in a nearly instinctive way in their achievements.

preface

Whether the author is aware of it or not, when a work of art causes emotion that is felt by everybody, its proportions are close to the golden section.

So then, why not use the help of drawings made according to the golden number to set the elements of the work together, whether it is a picture, an object or a building?

Phidias, Leonardo Da Vinci and the cathedral builders understood it.
That exercise is in itself sufficient to "educate" the eye.

Robert Vincent has had the remarkable idea of presenting us basic drawings, simple drawings, very often novel and very well commented on.

They can be made by all, youngsters or senior citizens, and be adapted to all forms of art or to all kinds of achievements or buildings made with passion.

Thanks to this "operative" geometry, I believe such a book will give all the creators of pictures and volumes the desire and the possibility of rediscovering the harmonious beauty of Nature, always to be found even in its most unusual elements.

And for those who do not create any work of art I hope they can find the picture and the explanation of the harmony resulting from the geometry of the Golden Section when they read this book or even just look at its pages which are so well illustrated.

Albert LeCoff, Philadelphia, 2003

* *The* ***Wood Turning Center*** *of Philadelphia (Pennsylvania USA) is a nonprofit membership organization, founded in 1986, dedicated to the education, preservation and promotion of the art and craft of lathe turning through the acquisition of collections and organization of exhibitions, conferences, a residency program, symposia and outreach programs.*

The Center's goal is to encourage and promote the work of established and developing artists and to cultivate, among the public, a deeper understanding and appreciation of lathe turned art.
Wood Turning Center 501 Vine Street Philadelphia, PA 19106 website: www.woodturningcenter.org

foreword

This book, entitled *"Geometry of the Golden Section"* might just as well have been entitled *"Discovery of the Treasures of Geometry"*, *"Lines Drawn by Ruler and Compass"*, *"The Dynamics of Number 5"* or also *"The Art of Lines"*.

Treasures, because we use the Golden Section that is the canon of Beauty and Harmony.

The knotted rope*, the stakes, the builders' stick and the plumbline have, among other devices, allowed our ancestors to draw semi-circles, straight lines and perpendiculars...all of them being the basic elements in the building of monuments that we still admire.

In this book, we use a ruler and a pair of compass to make such geometrical figures.

Indeed, our purpose is to study the aesthetic properties of geometry according to the golden section determined not by calculation but only by drawing.

About one hundred geometric figures, **many of them quite novel**, are proposed to help the reader acquire the art of line drawing.

That technique, specifically based on arithmetic and geometric ratios, was that of the Romanesque builders and their Egyptian, Chaldean and Greek predecessors (in those days decimal numbers, trigonometry and even the signs for addition, multiplication and division were unknown).

* see page 35

It is a well known fact that it was only during the Italian Renaissance, in the 14th and 15th centuries, that the use of Arabic numerals, among which "zero", became common.

This study will help young people, who use computers and calculators more and more, to sharpen their intuition and develop their taste for research.

It will also give senior citizens a way to keep their minds young and enrich their retirement years.

Let everyone discover, by the art of geometric figures, in particular those of line drawing, the treasures inspired by the Golden Section.

Isn't geometric drawing an activity that requires all one's knowledge and stimulates one's imagination and reflection?

Every one will therefore be able to verify by his own experience that mathematical knowledge is not necessary to build geometric figures .

One can draw many figures that are beautiful and attractive just by means of a ruler and compass.

I have written a little book entirely dedicated to the creation of such drawings: "Nombre d'Or et Créativité" Chalagam edition 2001.

Pascal said: *"We can see by experience that given equal minds and all things similar, he who has a geometrical mind gets the upper hand and acquires a new strength."*

ACKNOWLEDGMENTS

I wish to thank all my friends that have helped me in many ways.
This is indeed a team work book.

Marie-Rose MAURIN, Reine NOBIO, Henri BILHEUST, Alain CARADEC, Robert CHALAVOUX, Robert GARÇON, Christian HAKENHOLZ, Guy MOURLEVAT, Michel REBOUL, Marc THÉROND, Jakub TROJANOWSKI, Gilbert ZOPPI.

Notes :

— Again, we point out that this book is a handbook of geometrical figures which can be useful for everyone's personal enrichment and which can prove, if need be, that our ancestors were able to build the harmonious monuments we continue to admire, using only ruler and compass (knotted rope, stakes, builders' stick...).

— When drawing a figure, follow the explanation and the drawing simultaneously.

— Each figure is given without any mathematical justification but we can supply it to those who would be interested.

It is up to the curious reader to have the pleasure of making the demonstration with the help of a few basic mathematical notions.

Such figures can also be the object of interesting problems.

— We have not represented the drawings related to hearts, spades, clubs, etc. nor the writing of capital letters as mentionned in PACIOLI's book.
They would have been superfluous in this book.

— When a point is defined by the intersection of two objects there may be a confusion if the two objects have several points of intersection: in such a case, the drawing is there to make things clear.

— By pedagogical desire, we have deliberately reused the same geometrical figures in different drawings (thus enabling the reader to get more familiar with the use of ruler and compass).

— Most figures use simple constructions resulting from the basic figures of chapter 1.

— The figures are, for most of them, the result of approximate methods. However, being hand-drawn, this result can be admitted as it is.

By simple mathematical calculation, using trigonometry in particular, one can determine the degree of approximation.

— When we speak of a length that is equal to 1 or 2 we give the chosen unit.

— Use of knotted rope:
the knotted rope measures length in "cubits"*
i.e. the distance between two knots.

Thus to determine :

- the value of $\Phi = 1.618...$ » 8/5, we use a rope of 8 + 5 = 13 "cubits" (2-13 page 20)
- the triangle 3-4-5, we use a rope of 3 + 4 + 5 = 12 "cubits" (1-10 page 20)
- the golden rectangle, we use one of the previous ropes.

You will notice that in the very dimensions of this book we have taken Φ into account: indeed, when open, the book is a golden rectangle: 42 cm long and 26 cm large, that is to say the Φ ratio.
(42 / 26 = 1.615) and each page has a ratio of approximately 26 / 21 = 1.272 = $\sqrt{\Phi}$.

* – (See page 32)

the golden section

When the different parts of a whole have harmonious ratios between each other and the totality, one can speak of BEAUTY and of HARMONY.

Nature has invented such proportions in Creation, and Man by intuition, has recognized them.

That beauty, that harmony spring from the ratio between the length and the width of a rectangle or between the height and the depth of a nave... and it so happens that this ratio, so often present, is the golden section "Φ" also called the golden number or divine proportion.

Thanks to it the artists of the 5th century B.C. caused the spectators' emotion: that very same emotion, that extraordinary impression of purity for the eye and for the mind, is to be felt in front of an abbey, a cathedral or a simple village church, built in the Middle Ages.

If, by luck, the stones of the building resound to music such as Gregorian chant, one's feelings cannot be expressed.

what is the golden section?

Φ, the golden section, the golden number, the divine proportion are synonymous expressions that define an arithmetical ratio.

That number is not a measure, nor a size.
It is a ratio between two homogeneous dimensions.

Thus, the golden section is the value of a ratio determined by a proportion.

A proportion is the equality between two ratios that are generally composed of four elements:
a, b, c, d. example: (a / *b* = c / d).

HOW TO CALCULATE THE GOLDEN SECTION*

The Golden section comes from a ratio that comprises only two elements such as

a / b = (a + b) / a

It is what is called in French "the principle of economy".
This proportion leads us to a second degree equation.
Indeed if we set a / b = Φ

we get $\Phi^2 - \Phi - 1 = 0$

This equation has a positive root:

$(1 + \sqrt{5}) / 2 = 1.618...$ (the value of Φ)

A golden rectangle is a rectangle that has a ratio of length over width equal to the F number.

Vitruvius (Roman architect, 1st century B.C.) gave the following definition of the value of Φ:
"Three points in line, determining two segments, form a golden section if there is between the small part and the longer one the same ratio as there is between the longer one and the whole"
["b" is the small part, "a" is the longer one, "a + b" is the whole. Thus $\frac{a}{b} = \frac{a+b}{a}$]

It is the parting of a line segment according to "mean and extreme ratio", called so by Euclid because the product of the "extremes" is equal to the product of the "mean" $\left(\frac{a}{b} \times \frac{(a+b)}{a}\right)$, which with a = F and b = 1 gives $F^2 = F + 1$, an equation that is the Φ "ratio" = 1.618...

* see Christian Hakenholz " Nombre d'Or et mathématique
Chalagam edition 2001

The golden section, called F since the beginning of the 20th century, is an irrational number in connection with the classical problem of the division of a line segment according to mean and extreme ratio.

It has quite a remarkable place in the infinite series by belonging simultaneously to two very well-known sequences of terms:

1- The Fibonacci numbers, an unending sequence 1 1 2 3 5 8 13 21 34 55 89 ...where each term is defined as the sum of its two predecessors.

2- A geometric sequence or geometric progression that is a series of numbers where a term is the product of the previous number by a set number that is called the common ratio of the sequence. Example: 1 2 4 8 16 32 ... common ratio = 2

-The Fibonacci numbers depend on the first two terms.
-The geometrical sequence depends on its first term and on the common ratio.

Can a geometric sequence be of Fibonacci?
Yes, on one condition only: that its common ratio be F

Example: 1 Φ Φ^2 Φ^3 Φ^4...
or,
... $1/\Phi^4$ $1/\Phi^3$ $1/\Phi^2$ $1/\Phi$ 1...

Φ = 1.618 ...
Φ^2 = 2.618...
$1/\Phi$ = 0.618...

It comes from the definition of F that is a number such as $\Phi + 1 = \Phi^2$ or such as $\Phi - 1 = 1/\Phi$

In other words, by adding 1 to Φ one obtains its square root and by subtracting 1 from Φ one obtains the reverse. (surprising , isn't it ?)

For the Fibonacci sequences that are not geometrical, the ratio between two consecutive terms is close to Φ, (8/5 = 1.6), (21 / 13 = 1.615) (89/55 = 1.6181) (144 / 89 = 1.6179) ....
Which is just as surprising, isn't it?

In a book entitled "The Divine Proportion" where he studies Euclid's Elements (3rd century B.C) PACIOLI (end of 15th century) declares that the effects of the divine proportion are: "numerous and marvellous, essential, admirable, supreme, most excellent, etc." (Today, we would say: fabulous! super!).

history of the golden section

Antiquity

Building has always been Man's great ambition and the discovery of the golden section probably dates back to the period of Antiquity.

The golden section can be found more than twenty times in the five ray star. Indeed, it is a symbol of it, along with the pentagon.

Number five is to be found in the Φ equation, thus establishing their relationship.

The division by five has been suggested by the great variety of five petal flowers (pentamerous), the five arms of a starfish, the pentagonal structure of the sea urchin and its five teeth...

Let's also note that Man has got 5 fingers (x 2), five toes (x 2) and five senses which are pentagonal representations. Number 5 brings about a relationship with Φ, that we would call the "dynamics of 5".

If the monuments prior to the Hellenic civilisation, specially those of Ancient Egypt (the CHEOPS pyramid is 47 centuries old), reveal the empirical use of the golden section, the texts describing its properties,or rather the geometrical figures pertaining to it, will only appear with the Greeks.

EUCLID, PYTHAGORAS and many others will give mathematical rigor to the golden section.

Three centuries B.C, EUCLID with his "Elements", offers a major contribution thanks to a geometrical demonstration: he built an isosceles triangle in which the value of each of the angles at the basis is double that of the remaining angle (in such an isosceles triangle the angle at the basis is worth 72° and the vertex angle is worth 36°).

Let's also note that 72° equals 1/5th of 360° and 36° is 1/10th of 360°: such angles are to be found in a regular pentagon.

From that triangle, EUCLID deduces how to build the regular pentagon, by observing that the diagonals of that pentagon intersect according to mean and extreme ratio and that the ratio of the diagonal to the side is equal to F.

He ends his "*Elements*" by inscribing in a sphere the **five** regular, platonic solids: tetrahedron, octahedron, isocahedron,hexahedron (cube), dodecahedron.

Reflecting on the golden section, VITRUVIUS (Roman architect 1st century B.C.) comes to the following conclusion: *"As the members of the body correspond to each other so must the parts of a building".*

Middle Ages

In the 11th and 12th centuries, at a time when stone testified to religious faith, 80 cathedrals were built, mainly in France, along with 500 large churches in monastries and towns, not to forget the tens of thousands of parochial churches.
It is the period of Romanesque Art: geometrical forms, light and sound vibrations are in harmony to reproduce the model of the Universe, celebrating the Creator's greatness.

At the end of the Romanesque period, there was an ever greater desire for elevation towards the sky and the light; cathedrals which were at first squat, started having higher and higher vaults thus giving birth to Gothic Art.

Gothic Art originated in France in the middle of the 12th century (the first gothic vault was built in 1144 in Saint Denis's Cathedral).

Gothic art is essentially characterized by the use of ribbed vaults, of the pointed arch instead of the round one and by the use of buttresses to support the main vault.

A cathedral is a stone book that exalts faith, harmony and beauty, just as Gregorian chant does -God's Word sung on splendid melodies.

Hence, it is medieval religious faith that is the real starting point of the "Cathedral Crusade".
That faith is at the same time a proof of love embodied in an architectural masterpiece where the *divine proportion* is largely present. Everything is at the same time symbol and geometry: symbolism of geometrical figures drawn essentially with ruler and compass according to the art of line tracing.

Renaissance

In the 15th century, "Euclid's Elements" were revived by Luca PACIOLI, a Fransciscan monk and theology teacher who knew very well through EUCLID and PYTHAGORAS the division of a straight line segment according to mean and extreme ratio.

His book, which we have already mentionned, deals with architecture, with the proportions of the human body and the letters of the alphabet.

This book was published again in 1988 by the "Librairie des Compagnons".

It is in Pacioli's time, i.e in the Renaissance, that great artists such as LEONARDO DA VINCI, adopted the *Divine Proportion* as the canon of Beauty and Harmony.

20th Century

Since the 20th century, the *Divine Proportion* has been represented by the letter Φ (PHI) by reference to PHIDIAS, the greatest and most famous artist that was at the same time a painter, an architect and a goldsmith in the 5th century B.C.

He built the Parthenon at Athens using the principles of harmony and beauty of the golden rectangle.

In 1931, Matila GHYKA wrote a very important book on the golden section. PAUL VALERY, LE CORBUSIER, CARTIER BRESSON, along with many others have underlined the major part played in Art by that number. LE CORBUSIER in particular, created his famous *"Modulor"* that he declared to be *"a work tool, a precise tool"*, or *"a keyboard, a piano, a well-tuned piano".*

Nowadays, the pyramid of the Louvre or the Geode (Paris) still bear witness to the presence of the golden section and many other surprising domains such as soccer or plastic surgery refer to it as the best equilibrium between the forms of the body or of the face.

presence of the golden section*

In Man

It has been observed since Antiquity that the architectural equilibrium of the human body is governed by the golden section.

The navel divides the body according to the golden section: it must correspond to the ratio between the total height of the body and the height of the navel to the ground.

Thus, when the Venus of Melos is seen in profile, considering the level of the foot arches, it is to be noted that the ratio between the total height of the statue and the distance separating the sole of the feet from the navel is equal to Φ.

It is again F that must regulate a harmonious ratio between the height and the width of a human head.

The latter example brings us back to Vitruve's canon of proportion, drawn by Leonardo Da Vinci in the 15th century, often used and still present nowadays, even in advertising.

In Nature

There is a great number of flowers that have 5 petals regularly placed (the pentamerous flower is inscribed in a regular pentagon).

At the heart of a sunflower, two networks of spirals are entwined, each one winding in a different way.

Those spirals, called "parastichies" have a characteristic: their numbers are equal to two consecutive terms of the Fibonacci series equaling 21 and 34, 34 and 55, or 55 and 89.

The iris flower, according to an article by Egbert STRILLER in the magazine Wedena of spring 1999, displays dimensions that are close to the Fibonacci numbers, a recurring series that is moreover of geometrical Φ means.

The case is similar for shells such as, in particular, the "Nautilus pompilius" in which geometrical spirals can be found by tracing a golden spiral.

In his book "DNA deciphered", Jean Claude FEREZ tells us: *"The thousands of nucleuses that compose the DNA are arranged according to numerical structures corresponding to the proportions of the Fibonacci numbers".*

The number of pairs of rabbits that could be bred by just one pair in a year's time has been calculated... and it has been found that it corresponds to a Fibonacci series with the golden number.

Marcel PAGNOL in his book "Jean de Florette" tells how he is going to *"prepare big crops, indispensable to the massive breeding of rabbits".*

Cut an apple into halves transversally (which is unusual) and you will observe the presence of a star-shaped pentagon and of a decagon.

In architecture

The CHEOPS pyramid (also called the "Great Pyramid"), built about 4700 years ago, is the golden pyramid (golden polyedre), in which many triangles containing number Φ can be found, particularly the ratio between the height of the triangular side to half the side of the square basis that is equal to $\sqrt{\Phi}$. You will discover others in chapter VI about line-tracing in human works.

Number Φ is to be found everywhere in many Romanesque and Gothic buildings.

In the medieval iconography of the Universe

A French artist of the 13th century represented God in the Genesis (The Great Architect) creating the Universe with compass (Miniature of the Vienna Bible, Austria, to be seen in this book on page 14). As in many other illuminations of that period, it is to be noted that the artist deliberately used in his miniature ratios and angles based on the golden section.

Many other examples can be provided to show the presence of the golden section in all domains. That presence can be natural, unconscious or carefully calculated.

Other harmonious proportions exist in nature and in human works but the "divine proportion" is undoubtedly the one that has, since the remotest ancient times, incited Man to look for beauty in harmony with himself and with Nature.

*the book by Robert Chalavoux "Nombre d'or ,nature et oeuvre humaine " Chalagam edition 2001 gives a lot of new and convincing examples of that presence.

In the measure instruments and the measurements used by the Romanesque builders.

The measure instruments:

— the builders' stick.
— the builders' "quine" (the five basic units of measurement).
— the 5 arm articulated instrument (similar to our wooden folding ruler with 5 arms, each 20 cm long).
— the Egyptian measurers' set square.
— the 12 "cubit" rope (12 intervals).
— the level and the plumbline.

The measurements: (see p 32 and 35)

When one wants to estimate a length, one often uses either the hand, the foot or the step; for example, the hand has determined the "empan" (the length between the extremity of the thumb and that of the little finger when the hand is stretched out) which allows one to measure a small length such as that of a table.

For the Romanesque builders' measurements, in France, the basic element was the "ligne" (line). However its value was not fixed and could vary from one builder to another.
The following equivalents are generally accepted:

The "ligne" (line) is worth 2.25 mm (it would correspond to the diameter of a barley grain !).
The "pouce" (inch) is worth 12 lignes (2.7 cm).
The "paume" (handbreadth or palm) is worth 34 lignes (7.64 cm = $1/\Phi^2$).
The "palme" is worth 55 lignes (12.36 cm = $1/\Phi$).
The "empan" is worth 89 lignes (20 cm = 1).
The "pied" (foot) is worth 144 lignes (32.36 cm = Φ).
The "coudée" (cubit) is worth 233 lines (52.36 cm = Φ^2).

The French "palme" does not correspond to the English "palm". Therefore we have kept the French spelling. No translation has been found either for "empan".

(the presence of the Fibonacci numbers is to be noted in the coefficients of conversion).

The "toise" (an old French unit of length equivalent to 1.949 meter) and the inch are not given here according to the golden number but they could be, as the "toise" is worth 6 feet (=194.16 cm) and the foot is equivalent to 12 inches of 12 lines.

Note:

6 cubits of 0.5236 m correspond to 3.1416...= π
3 feet of 0.3236 m are worth about one meter.
The handbreadth and the palme, the empan, the foot and the cubit (the five elements constituting the builders' "quine") bear reference to human dimensions and at the same time to Φ, the golden section, the golden number or the divine proportion.

WITH THE GOLDEN NUMBER EVERYTHING IS BEAUTY AND HARMONY

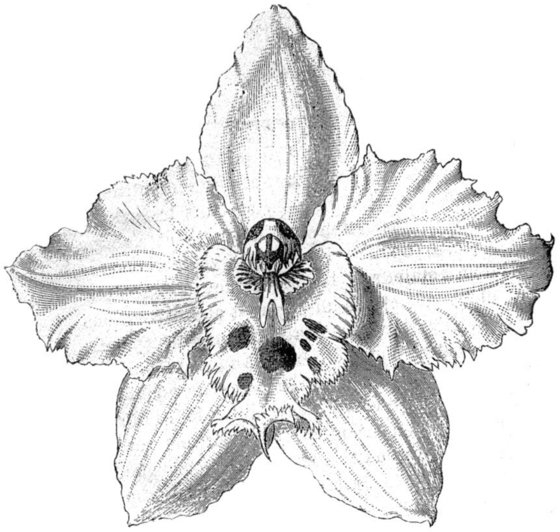

Orchid, fig.1555 *le Monde entier des plantes*
of Paul Constantin Librairy J.B. Baillière Paris 1896

13th century Vienna Bible

God in the Genesis

The artist who achieved this work of art has deliberately set relationships between the symbolical representations of the elements of his composition.

According to Guy Mourlevat, by using a proportion compass one can find the F ratio between:

— the length of the leg of the compass (from the hinge to the tip) and God's left eye to the hinge.
— the length of the leg of the compass and the diameter of the circle that is the orbit of the centers moon / sun.
— the diameter of the aureole and the distance between the sun and the moon.
— the distance from the center of the aureole to the center of the universe and the diameter of the universe.
— the diameter of the universe and the diameter of the aureole.

The length of the vertical leg of the compass is equal to the length of God's step (from heel to heel). The author of this book has checked those data and has come to the same conclusions.

GEOMETRICAL LINE-TRACING

The following seven chapters start with the chapter on **basic figure-tracing**
Chapter 1 contains figures that are often referred to by their number followed by that of the page: example (1-09 page 22).

For all the figures in the book that you wish to draw:

the data are indicated by a long dashed line – – – – – – – – – – – – – –
the construction lines by a thin continuous line ————————————
the final result by a continuous thick line ━━━━━━━━━━━━
the symmetry axes by a dash-dotted line –·–·–·–·–·–·–·–·–·–
the special lines by a thick or thin line different from the previous ones: for example --

Mathematical knowledge is not necessary to draw any of the figures as in the time of the ancient builders who did not even know points (such as in 0.5 cm for example).

However, we will indicate the relationships deriving from the very well-known theorems of Pythagoras or Thales, to make the figures easier to understand and more interesting.

To help the readers who wish, at all costs,to make calculations, we indicate the value of the angles with their sine and cosine, ... according to the golden section (which is indispensable to estimate the approximations, or for further investigations, but not necessary at all to draw the figures).

Now, it is up to you to discover how interesting the "divine proportion" and the "dynamics of number 5" can be.

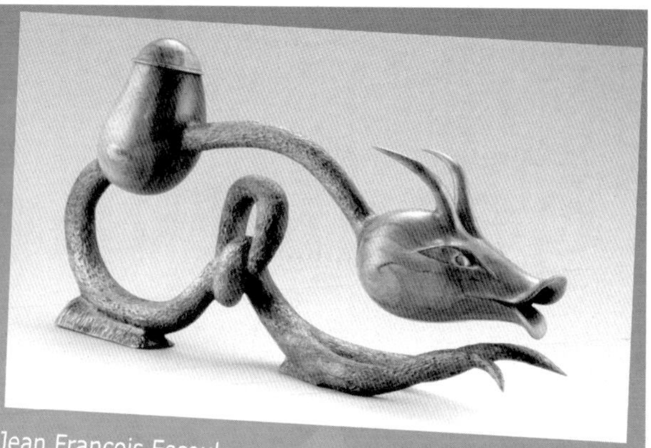

Jean François Escoulen **contemporary** French Woodturner

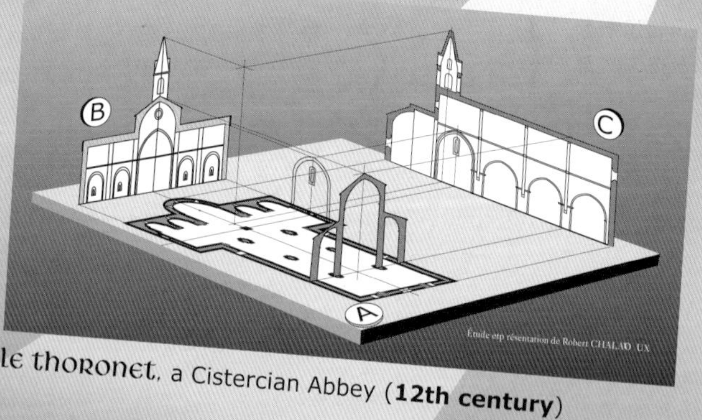

le thoronet, a Cistercian Abbey (**12th century**)

Stephanoceras, a **fossil**

natural proportion
from nature to art

Finding pentagons and pentagrams in Nature

BASIC FIGURES

1

FIG. 1-01 ~ TRACING THE SYMMETRY OF A POINT TO A STRAIGHT LINE

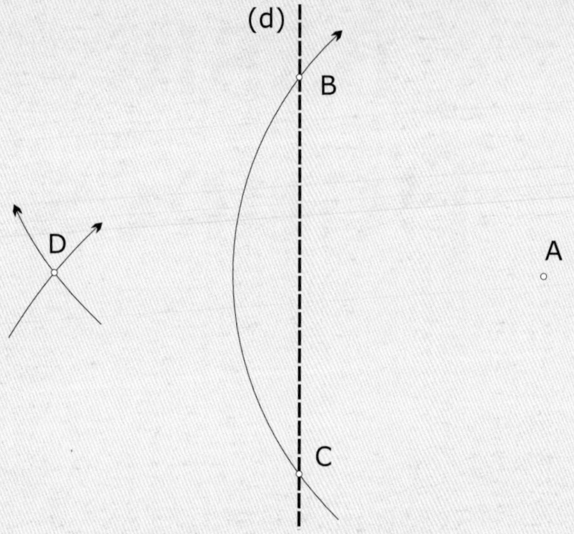

Consider point A and straight line (d).

Draw the arc of a circle with A as center that intersects (d) at C and B.

Draw the arc of a circle with B as center, BA as radius then draw the arc with C for center and the same radius. Those two arcs intersect at D.

D, is the symmetrical point to A in relation to (d).

Note: AD is perpendicular to BC: hence it is easy to deduce how to draw the perpendicular to a straight line (d) passing by point A.

FIG. 1-02 ~ CONSTRUCTING THE MEDIAN AND THE MIDDLE OF A SEGMENT

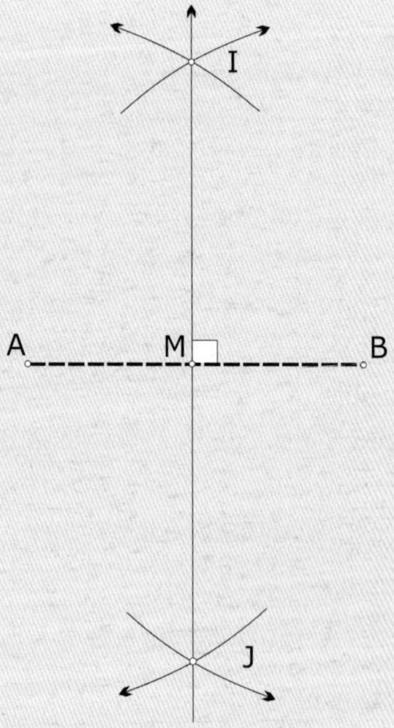

Consider line segment AB.

Draw an arc with A for center and with a long enough radius.

Draw an arc with B for center and with a similar radius.

These two arcs intersect at I and J.

The straight line passing by points I and J is the median of AB.

Line I J intersects the A B line segment in its middle.

Fig. 1-03 ~ constructing a perpendicular to a straight ligne passing by a point situated on that line.

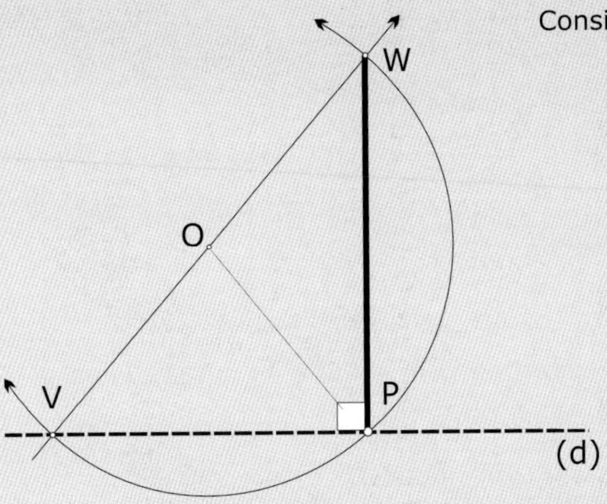

Consider the straight line (d) and point P situated on that line.

Take an O point at random.

Draw an arc with O for center and OP for radius intersecting (d) at another point : V.

Draw the straight line VO intersecting the circle that has O for center at W.

P W is perpendicular to (d) passing by P.

Notes: – Two lines perpendicular to (d) are parallel to each other.

– To draw a parallel to a straight line from an exterior point P, one has only to draw the perpendicular of P to this straight line and to translate this distance from another point of the straight line (1-07 p 21).

Fig. 1-04 ~ triangle 3-4-5 and its particularities

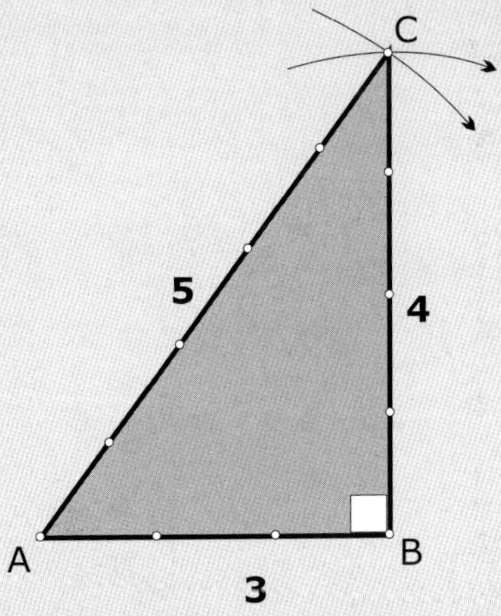

Triangle 3-4-5, also called the "familiar triangle 3-4-5", is always a right angle triangle.

Indeed, AB = 3 and BC = 4, the sum of the squares of the sides: (3 x 3) + (4 x 4) = 9 + 16 = 25, which is the square of AC (5 x 5) according to the theorem of Pythagoras, the triangle is right angled at B.

To draw it, one has simply, starting from AB = 3: to draw from A an arc with a radius = 5 and from B an arc with a radius = 4. These two arcs intersect at C.

Note: This triangle was often the basis of the builders' plans: it made it easier for them to place perpendiculars and parallels.

Fig. 1-05 ~ construction of the bisector of an angle

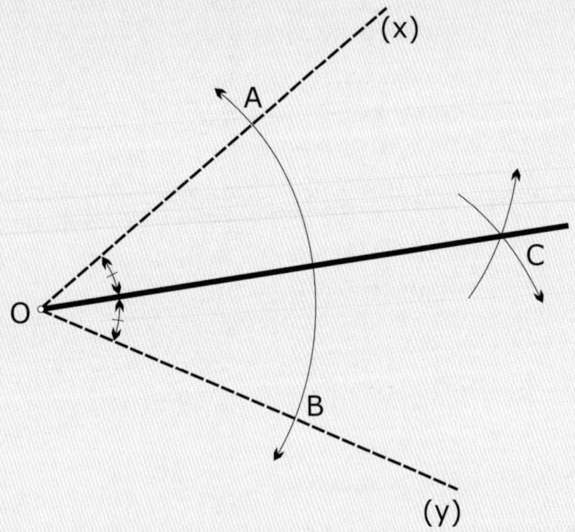

Consider angle xOy.

Draw an arc with O as center,

cutting the semi-straight line Ox at A

and the semi-straight line Oy at B.

Starting from A and B as centers, draw

two arcs with a similar radius that cut at C.

OC is the bisector of angle xOy.

Fig. 1-06 ~ drawing the arc "capable" of a line segment under a specified angle

Consider line segment BC and an A angle.

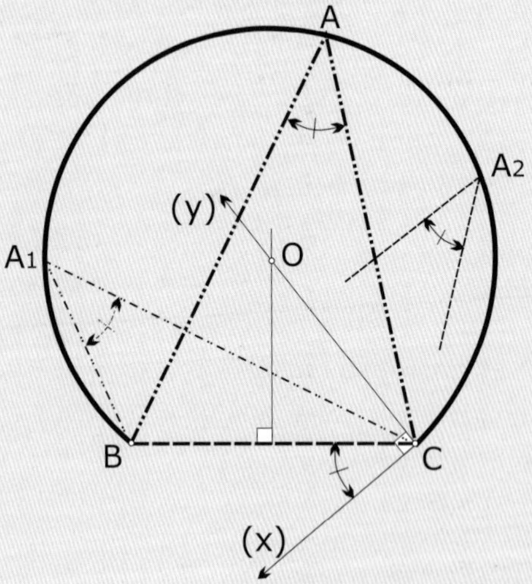

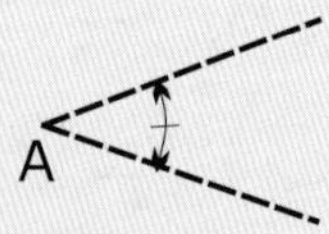

Draw a straight line Cx forming with BC an angle
that is equal to A.

Draw the perpendicular to Cx at point C (that is Cy).

Draw the median of BC intersecting Cy at O.

Draw the arc that has O for center and OC for radius.

You have thus determined the BC arc of line segment
BC under angle A.

From all the points of the BC arc (whether A, A_1, A_2...)
the BC line segment can be "seen" from the same A angle.

FIG. 1-07 ~ DRAWING SIMILAR TRIANGLES (THALES: 600 B.C.)

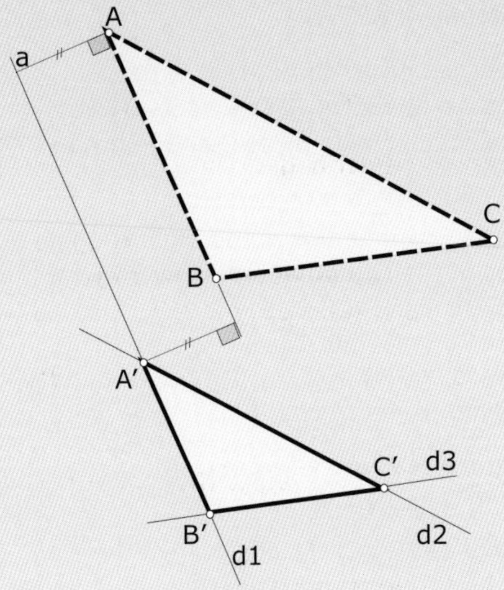

Consider triangle ABC
From an A' point, draw aA', (d1) parallel to AB then d2 parallel to AC.

From a point on d1, B' for example, draw a line parallel to BC intersecting d2 at C'.

The A'B'C' triangle is similar to the ABC triangle.
The two triangles have equal corresponding angles.

The Thales theorem:

Any parallel to one of the sides of a triangle divides the two other sides according to the same ratio.
Let's translate triangle A'B'C' onto ABC with A' onto A and B' onto AB (C' will be on AC):

According to Thales we shall have:
AB / AB' = AC / AC' = BC / B'C'

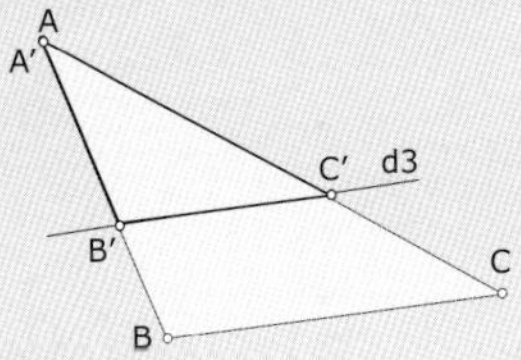

Note:– This theorem is often applied to the golden triangles.
–Thank to it in the past it was possible to measure the height of a pyramid or of a tower by the length of their shadow compared to the shadow of a vertical stick of a known length.

FIG. 1-08 ~ DIVIDING A LINE SEGMENT INTO "N" EQUAL PARTS

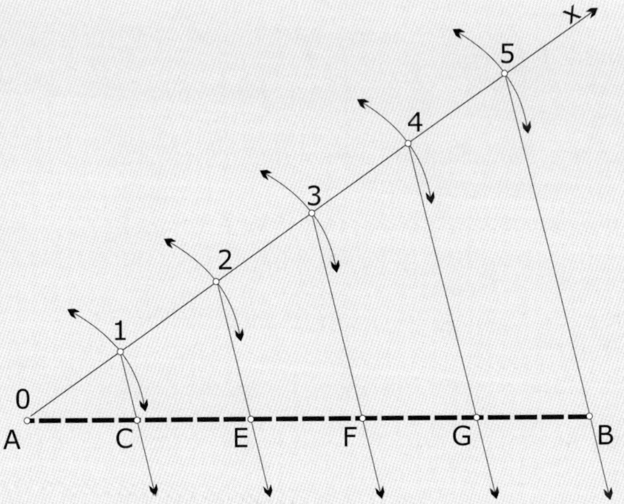

Consider line segment AB to be divided into "n" equal parts with, for example, n = 5

From point A draw an Ax straight line then from A with any compass opening translate this opening 5 times onto Ax.

From point 5, join B.

Draw the parallel lines to 5B passing by points 1,2,3,4.

Points C,E,F and G divide AB into 5 equal parts.

AC = CE = EF = FG = GB = AB / 5

Note: The figure is more precise when straight line Ax makes an angle between 30 and 50° and with a compass opening close to AB / 5.

Fig. 1-09 ~ the half L-shaped square and its characteristics.

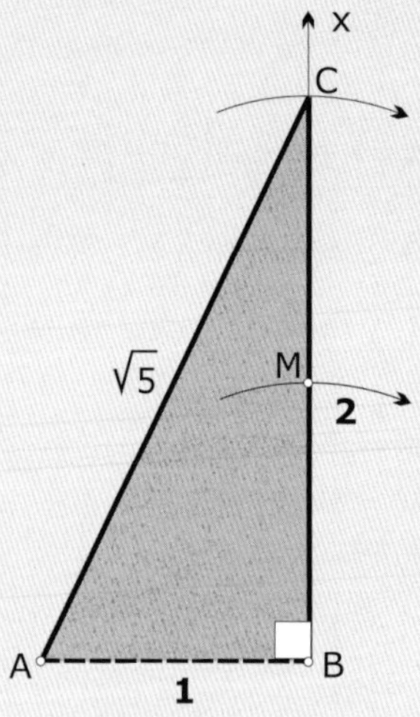

Consider line segment AB = 1

From point B draw a line perpendicular to AB, that is Bx.
Draw the arc with B as center and AB as radius. It intersects Bx at M.
From M, translate again this arc which intersects Bx at C and join A to C.

The 1/2 L-shaped square (ABC) is thus defined
Characteristic : The square of the AC hypotenuse of this right triangle is equal to the sum of the squares of the two other sides (Pythagoras)
hence : $1^2 + 2^2 = 5$ and AC = $\sqrt{5} = 2.236$

The builders had $\sqrt{5}$ on their L-shaped square and, by pivoting around A, they got the immediate measure of $1 + \sqrt{5}$

Thus, the **L-shaped square was very important** for the building Companions.

We see it very often in their drawings (ABC in 1-11 and many others...)
Note that the diagonal of the Barlong square (double square, 2-05 page 29) divides it into two 1/2 L-shaped squares.

Note: AB + AC = 1 + 2.236 = 2 Φ, a characteristic that is also used in some drawings

Fig. 1-10 ~ bisector of the angle of a triangle

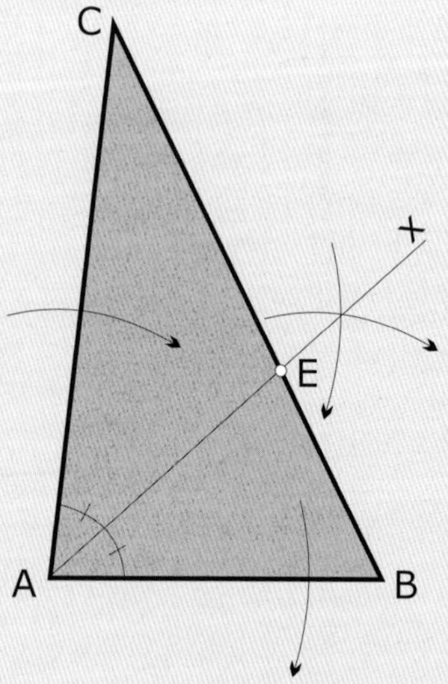

Consider triangle ABC.

Draw the Ax bisector of the A angle (1-05, page 20).

That line divides the BC side of the triangle into two segments CE and EB. Their ratio is equal to the ratio of the two adjacent sides AC and AB.
It is written : CE / EB = CA / AB
or also CE / CA = BE / BA.

Hence the theorem:

the bisector of the angle of a triangle divides the opposite side into two segments that are proportional to the adjacent sides.

Note: this theorem and the drawings that result from it are used when those ratios are precisely linked to the golden section such as in the acute and obtuse triangles.

FIG. 1-11 ~ DIVIDING A LINE SEGMENT ACCORDING TO MEAN AND EXTREME RATIO

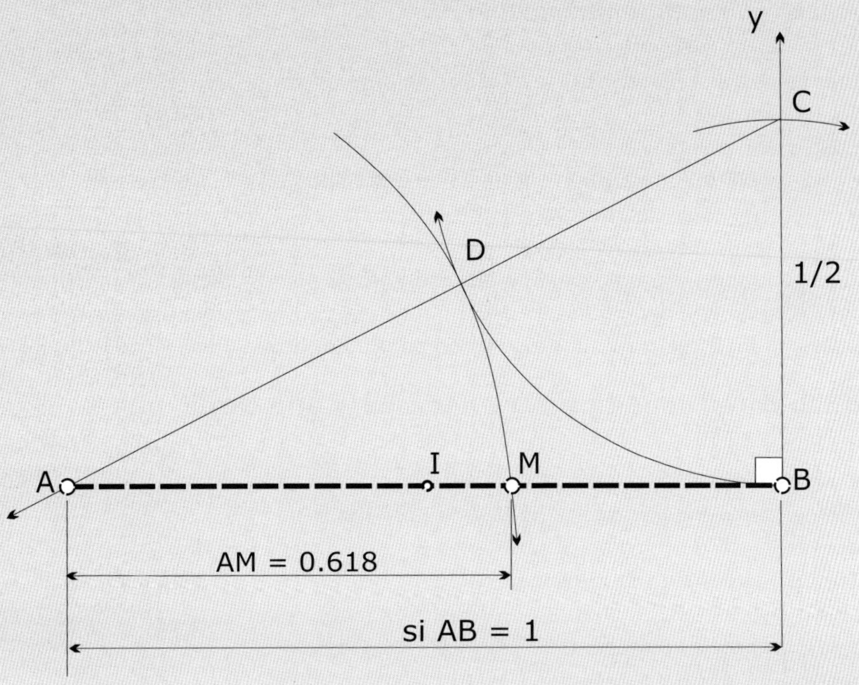

Consider line segment AB. Place I, the middle of AB (1-02 page 18)

From B, draw a line perpendicular to AB (1-03 page 19), that is By.

Draw an arc with B as center and BI = AB / 2 for radius that intersects By at C.

Draw line segment AC.

Draw an arc with C as center and CB as radius intersecting AC at D.

Draw an arc with A as center and AD as radius intersecting AB at M.

Point M divides the AB line segment according to mean and extreme ratio.

AM / MB = AB / AM = Φ = 1.618

MB / AM = AM / AB = 1 / Φ = 0.618

If AB is chosen as unit: AB = 1

then AM = 0.618 = 1/ Φ = Φ - 1

(it is easy to verify it on the figure and with 1 / 1.618 = 1.618 - 1)

Note: — the ABC triangle defines the 1/2 L-shaped square.

— That construction is very often used in our books of the "Golden Section" series.

FIG. 1-12 ~ DRAWING A GIVEN CIRCLE AND DRAWING CURVES

necessary and sufficient conditions

Let us recall that **to draw a straight line**, two conditions, two only are necessary.
For example:
— passing by two given points
— passing by a given point and parallel to a given straight line (1-07 and 1-08p. 21)
— being tangent to a given circle at a given point of this circle
— etc.
Just one of those conditions, passing by a point, would leave an infinite variety of solutions.
A supplementary condition is not necessary and might make it impossible to draw the figure.
For example: passing by three points if those three points are not in line.

FOR A CIRCLE: three conditions are necessary and three only

Examples:
— passing by three points A, B, C, that are not in line
Figure a : The center of the circle passing by points A and B is necessarily on the median of segment AB (1-02 p. 18) just as it is on the median of segment BC. The center is therefore O, the point of intersection of the two medians .

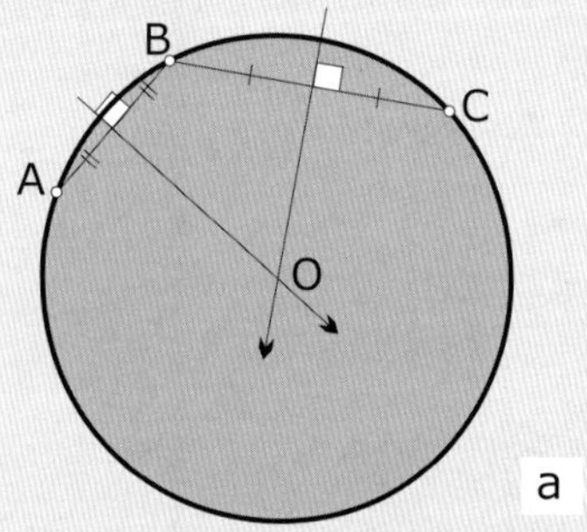

— being tangent to three staight lines d, d_1, d_2 in the same plane

figure b The center of the circle that is tangential to d and d_1 will necessarily be on the bisector of angle dMd_1 (1-05 p. 20). The same goes for angle d_1Nd_2.
The center is therefore point O, the intersection of the two bisectors. The points of tangency are determined by tracing from 0 the perpendiculars to the three straight lines (d,d_1,d_2).

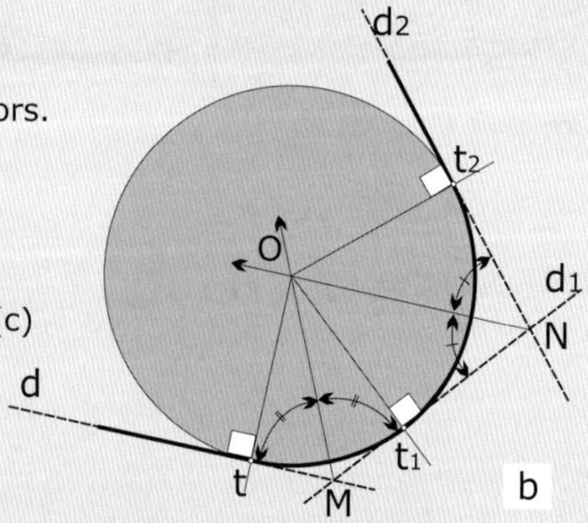

— Joining a given straight line (d) at a given point (p) of a circle (c)

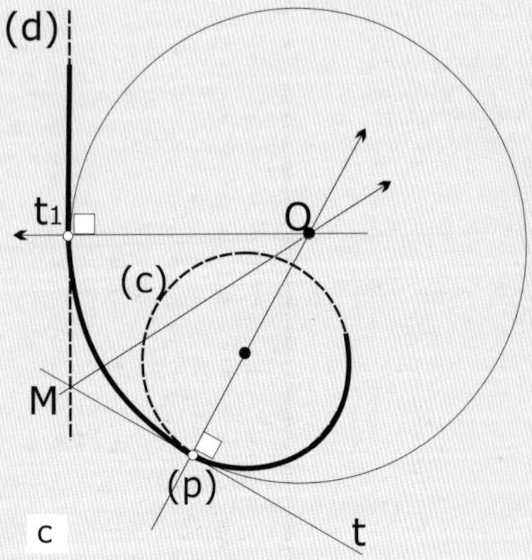

figure c : The 0 center that is to be found is necessarily situated on a **perpendicular to tangent** "t" of circle (c) and also on the bisector of angle dMt, hence the 0 center.
The points of tangency delimit with precision the staight lines and the arcs.

Note: — Two circles which are tangent at a same point necessarily have their centers **on the same perpendicular** to this tangent.
— If it was also required to draw the radius of the circle with 0 for center, the figure would be impossible because that radius is a result.

Creation

Graphic representation of the Golden number and its measure

2

Fig. 2-01 ~ Drawing a golden rectangle starting from the basic square

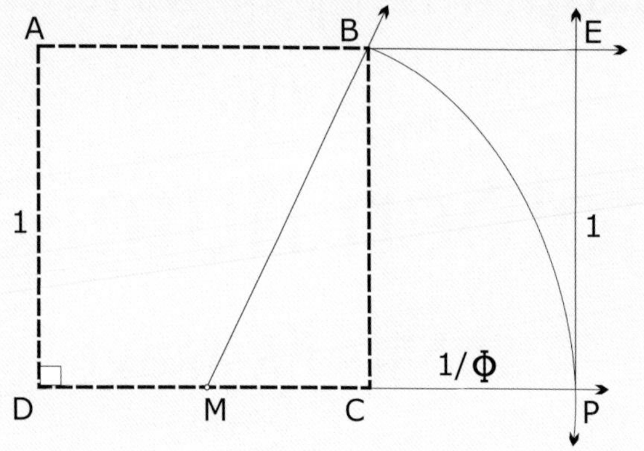

Consider an ABCD square, whose side = 1 unit. Place M in the middle of DC.

Draw the arc of a circle with M as center and MB as radius, cutting the straight line DC at point P.

DC / CP = DP / DC = Φ

Draw segment PE perpendicular to DC cutting line AB at point E.

Thus we obtain the golden rectangle AEPD as the ratio of the sides of the golden rectangle AEPD is: K = DP / AD = Φ

If AD = 1, then DP = Φ

The BEPC rectangle is also a golden rectangle.

Note: the golden rectangle is the only rectangle to possess that characteristic: if the square built in its width is suppressed, we get another rectangle of the same shape BEPC (length / width = Φ). Several figures in this book use that characteristic.

Fig .2-02 ~ Drawing the golden rectangle starting from the « musical quinte 3/2 »

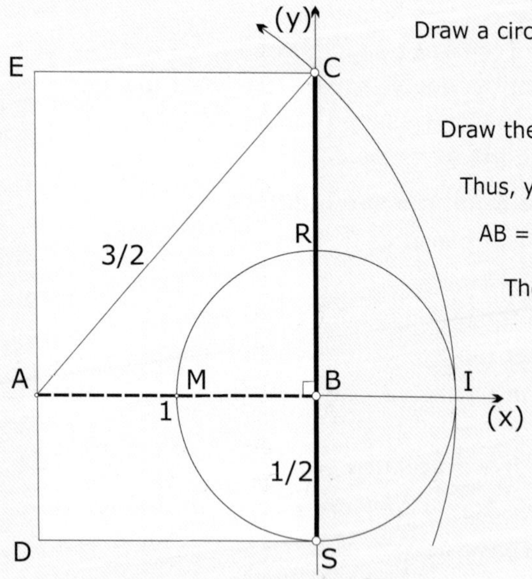

If AB = 1, so SC = Φ.

Consider line segment AB with M as middle point.

Draw a circle with B as center and BM as radius cutting AB at point I.

Draw By perpendicular to Ax at point B.

Draw the arc with A as center and AI as radius intersecting By at C.

Thus, you build the right triangle ACB that is right-angled at B such as AB = 1 and the hypothenuse AC is equal to the musical quinte 3/2.

The circle with B as center and BM as radius (already drawn) intersects By at points R and S.

SC / AB = Φ or AB = RS, hence SC / RS = Φ.

R cuts SC according to mean and extreme ratio:
RS / RC = SC / RS = Φ.

Draw rectangle DECS, hence CS = ED and DS = AB:

DECS is a golden rectangle.

fig. 2-03 ~ drawing the golden section starting from triangle 3-4-5

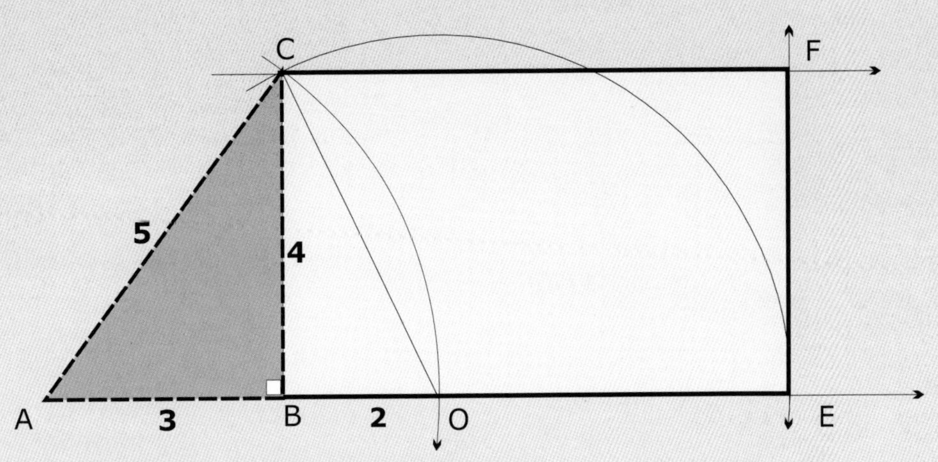

Consider the familiar triangle ABC right angled at B such as:
AB = 3, BC = 4 and AC = 5.

Draw the arc with A as center and AC as radius that intersects AB at O.
Draw the arc with O as center and OC as radius that intersects AB at E.

$BE / BC = \Phi$

From point E draw a line perpendicular to EB, then from point C a line perpendicular to CB.
The two perpendiculars intersect at F thus forming the golden rectangle EBCF.

The ratio of the sides is equal to Φ

if side EF = 1, side BE = Φ

Note: AC = AO as the radius is the same and BO = 5 - 3 = 2.
Triangle BCO is a half L-shaped square 1 /2 (as BO = BC / 2).

Another construction can be made with a ½ L-shaped square :

Consider a 1/2 L-shaped square, BCO, with BO = 1
From O, draw the arc with an OC radius that intersects the continuation of BO at E
BE = BO + OC or $OC = \sqrt{5}$ **hence $BE = 1 + \sqrt{5}$**
and as BC = 2, we get $BE / BC = (1 + \sqrt{5}) / 2 = \Phi$.

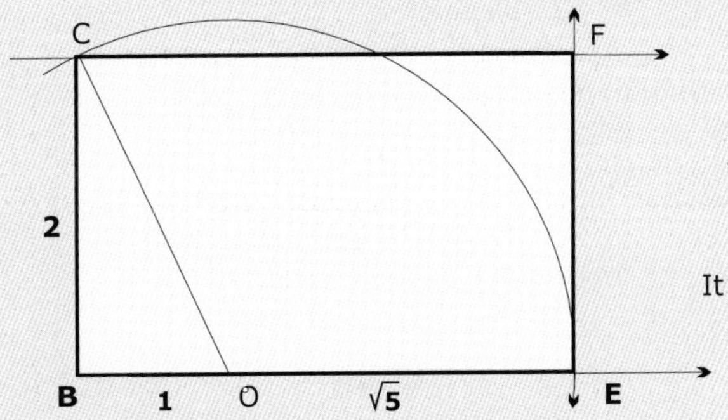

By this very simple figure with the 1/2 L-shaped square, the golden rectangle can be defined, so can the golden section by the ratio of its sides BE / BC.

It is the graphic illustration of the calculation of the golden section on page 9.

Fig. 2-04 ~ Drawing a golden rectangle starting from the 1/2 L-shaped square

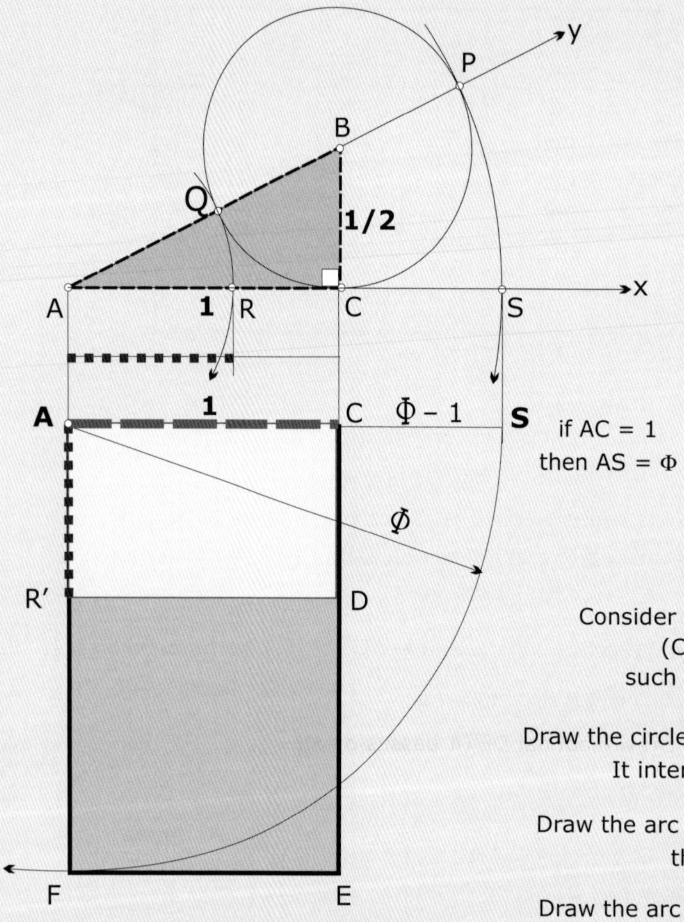

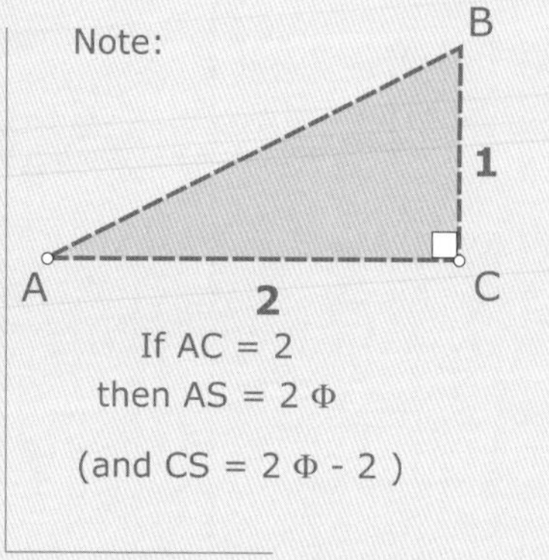

Consider the 1/2 L-shaped square ABC,
(C being the right angle)
such as: AC = 1 and BC = 1/2.

Draw the circle with B as center and BC as radius.
It intersects Ay at points P and Q.

Draw the arc with A as center and AQ as radius
that intersects Ax at R.

Draw the arc with A as center and AP as radius
that intersects Ax at S.

R divides the AC line segment according to mean and extreme ratio
AR / RC = AC / AR = Φ.
It is the basic figure 1-11 on page 23, here this figure defines the sides
of the golden rectangle ACDR′ with AR′ = AR.

C divides the AS line segment according to mean and extreme ratio
AC / CS = AS / AC = Φ,
hence the figure of the golden rectangle ACEF.

The construction obtained by assembling the two golden rectangles,
defined by the 1/2 L=shaped square, is the same as that of figure 2-01 page 26.

FIG. 2-05 ~ DRAWING A GOLDEN RECTANGLE STARTING FROM THE DOUBLE SQUARE, (ALSO CALLED BARLONG SQUARE)

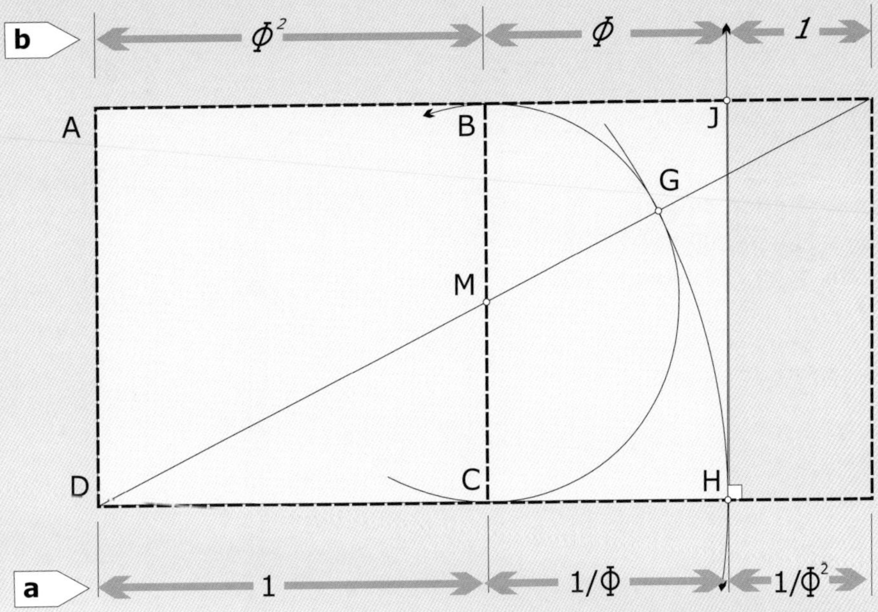

Consider two joint squares ABCD and BEFC, side = 1 unit.

Place M in the middle of BC.

Draw diagonal DE (it passes by M)

Draw an arc with M as center and BC /2 as radius that intersects DE at G.

Draw an arc with D as center and DG as radius that intersects DF at H.

From H draw the perpendicular that intersects AE at J.

a — Considering DCHF with DC = 1

C divides the DH line segment according to mean and extreme ratio: $DC / CH = DH / CH = \Phi$

and $CH / DC = 1 / \Phi$ As $DC = 1$, $CH = 1 / \Phi$

H divides line segment CF according to mean and extreme ratio: $CH / HF = CF / CH = \Phi$

so $HF / CH = 1 / \Phi$. as $CH = 1 / \Phi$, $HF = 1 / \Phi^2$.

(for DGHC, the figure is identical to APSC of 2-04 on the previous page).

b — *Considering ABJE with JE = 1.*

J divides line segment BE according to mean and extreme ratio: $BJ / JE = BE / BJ = \Phi$.

as $JE = 1$, $BJ = \Phi$

B divides line segment AJ according to mean and extreme ratio $AB / BJ = AJ / AB = \Phi$.

as $BJ = \Phi$, $AB = \Phi^2$

Note: As well as the golden rectangle AJHD, this figure also determines the elements of the "quine" (2-09 page 33)

FIG. 2-06 ~ the golden L-shaped square

The *proportion compass* has two movable legs, for which AB / CD is always equal to Φ whatever the opening width.

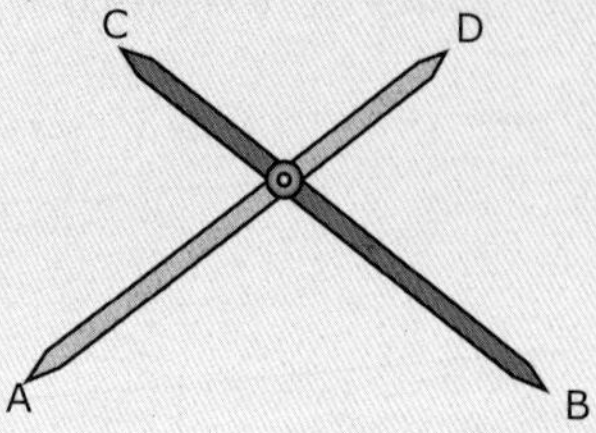

The golden L-shaped square indicates the $1 / \Phi$, $\sqrt{\Phi}$, Φ et Φ^2 ratios from any segment taken as unit.

Given the sliding arm Mx-My:

$$A\text{-}Mx = \sqrt{\Phi}$$
$$A\text{-}My = 1$$
$$Mx\text{-}My = \Phi$$
$$(Mx\text{-}My)+AMx = \Phi^2$$

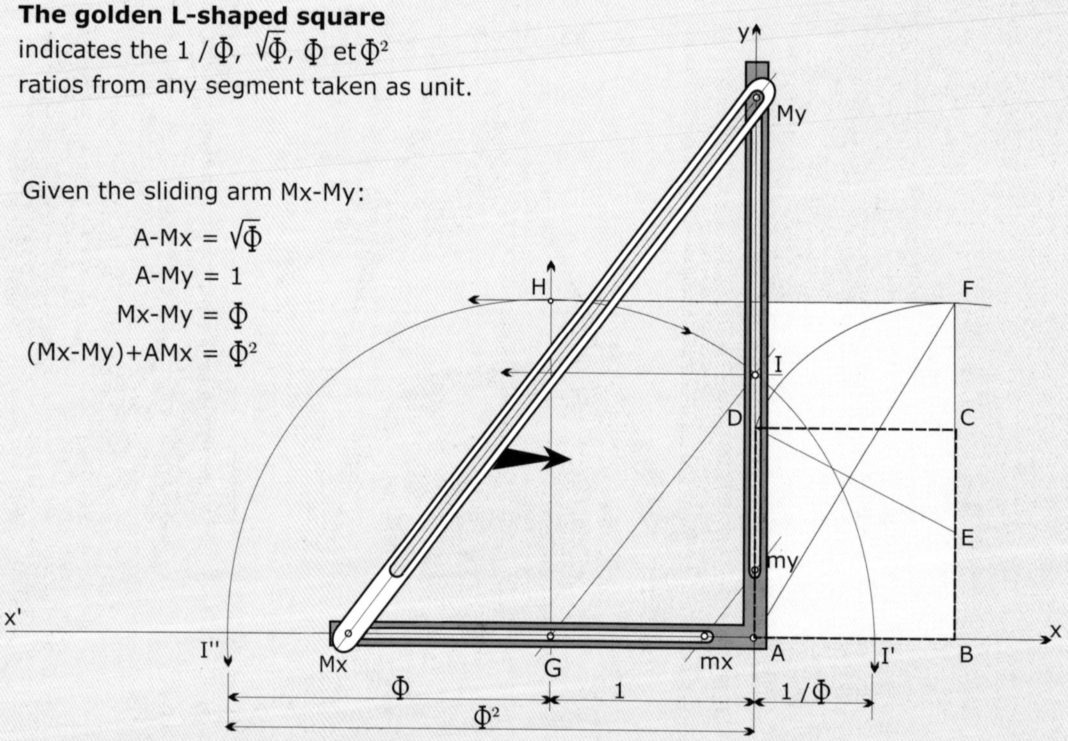

Consider axes Ax and Ay.

From the ADCB square, draw the golden rectangle with sides: AB = 1 and BF = Φ.

Place AG = AB = 1 on Ax'

From point G draw the perpendicular to Ax and from F the perpendicular to BF.

Those two straight lines intersect at H.

Draw the circle with a G center and a GH radius that intersects Ay at I.

The AGI triangle is such that AI $= \sqrt{\Phi}$, AG = 1, and GI = GI'' = Φ

When placed in position GI, by rotating on G, the sliding arm will indicate I'I'' = $\Phi^2 + 1 / \Phi = 2\Phi$

This instrument, built by the author himself, makes it possible to find quickly, by moving the sliding arm in a way parallel to itself, the Φ, $1 / \Phi$, $\sqrt{\Phi}$, Φ^2 values on an object or a picture according to AG = 1.

fig. 2-07 ~ le corbusier's "modulor"

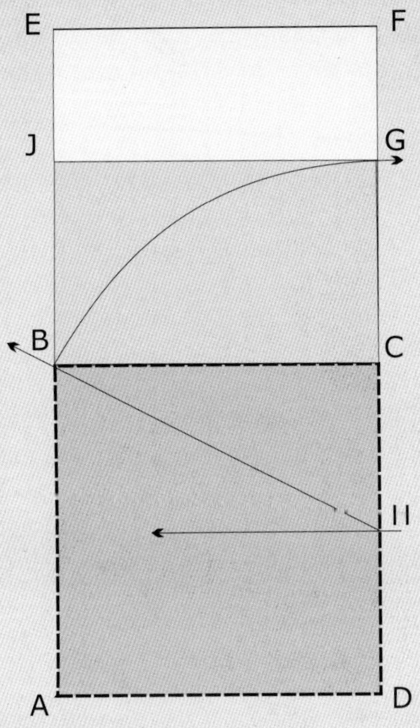

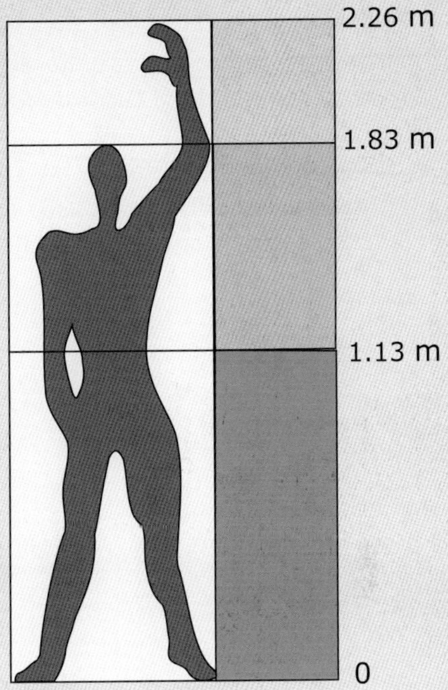

Le Corbusier was a French architect, urbanist and painter of Swiss origin (1887 - 1965). He constructed many buildings with reference to the human body as a module which he used as a basic unit for determining the dimensions of habitations such as the ones in the "Cité Radieuse" (the Happy City) in Marseille (South of France) in 1947. He called this module "the Modulor".

What is the Modulor?

By examining the drawing established according to his own dimensions, we can see that:

1.13 + 1.13 = 2.26 m: the rectangle AEFD is a "Barlong rectangle" (2-05 page 29)

1.83 / 1.13 = 1.619: that is 1, to say the golden section (nearest one-thousandth)

1.83 - 1.13 = 0.70 and 1.13/0.7 = 1.614 = Φ (nearest 4-thousandth).

The rectangle AJGD is a golden rectangle (2-01 page 26).

Le Corbusier then gave the dimensions of a man standing, leaning on his elbow, then sitting, and sitting leaning on his elbow.... and the ratio of dimensions is always

$1/\Phi$, $\sqrt{\Phi}$ Φ ou Φ^2.

He asserted that the "Modulor" had two advantages over the metric system by putting man at the center of architecture and by taking possession of space according to the laws that govern Nature.

FIG. 2-08 – MEASURING ELEMENTS USED BY THE ROMANESQUE BUILDERS

The measures that were chosen, by conveniency, according to the average size of a body and easy to verify, were: the "handbreadth", the "palme" (distance from the tip of the little finger to the tip of the forefinger), the "empan" (distance from the tip of the thumb to the tip of the little finger), the "foot", and the "cubit" (= "coudée").

According to the literature on measurements, it was the "cubit" (= "coudée" called the "royal cubit", which was used as reference for a coherent determination of the other dimensions linked to the geometric Fibonacci sequence (p.10 and 13).

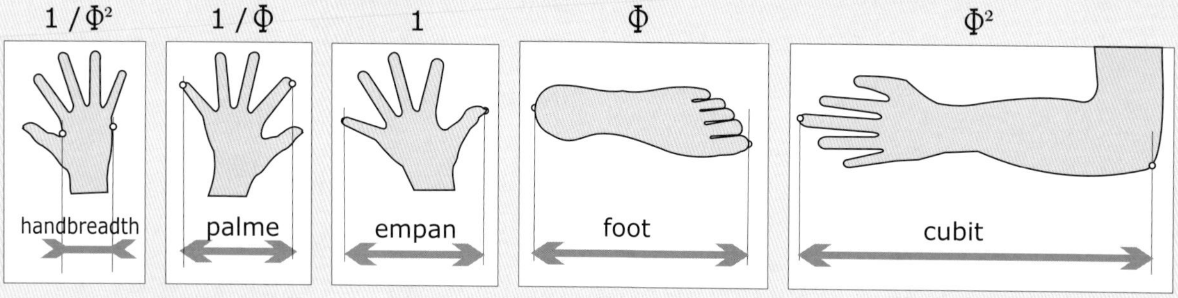

If the "empan" is taken as unit
the HANDBREADTH = 7.64 cm corresponding to $1 / \Phi^2$
the PALME = 12.36 cm corresponding to $1 / \Phi$
the EMPAN = 20 cm = 1
the FOOT = 32.36 cm corresponding to Φ
the ROYAL CUBIT = 52.36 cm corresponding to Φ^2
It also bears a relation to π.

π **/ 6** = 3.1416 / 6 = 0.5236 = the CUBIT (in meters)

According to the characteristics of the geometrical Fibonacci sequence
cubit / foot = foot / empan = empan / palme = palme / handbreadth = Φ

and

cubit = foot + empan
foot = empan + palme
empan = palme + handbreadth

Note: Today, an average cubit is inferior to 50 cm
which would suggest a biggish foot and small hands;
their cubit was indeed "royal"!

FIG. 2-09 ~ THE BUILDERS' "QUINE" AND THE STAR-SHAPED PENTAGON

The elements of measure are deduced from a regular pentagon.
The QUINE is the totality of these elements.

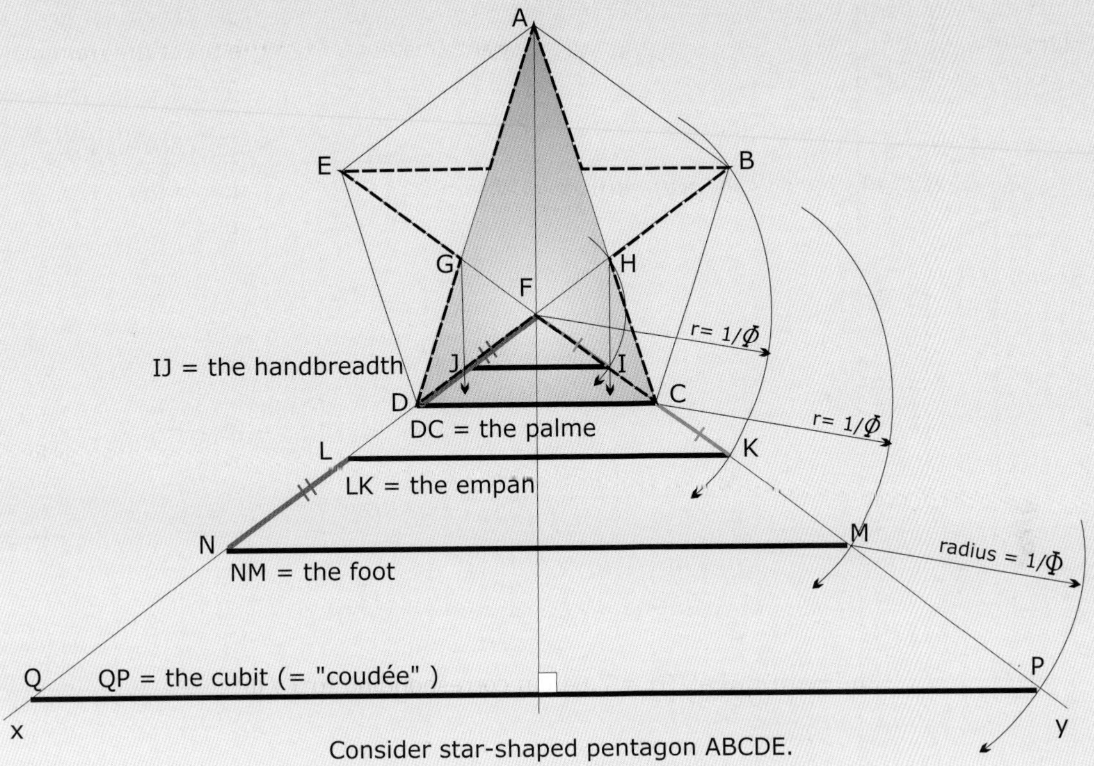

Consider star-shaped pentagon ABCDE.
the prolonged diagonals BDx and ECy intersecting at F,
diagonals EC and AD intersecting at G
and diagonals BD and AC intersecting at H.

The perpendicular line drawn from G onto DC (or r = FH) intersects BD at J.
The perpendicular line drawn from H onto DC intersects EC at I and
I J = $1 / \Phi^2$, it is the **HANDBREADTH** and DC =$1 / \Phi$ it is the **PALME.**
on Bx, place DL = FJ.
From L, draw the line parallel to DC that intersects Ey at K and LK = **1**: it is the **"EMPAN".**
(we have arbitrarily adopted the empan as unit 1, we might just as well
have chosen the palme or the cubit)**.**
On Bx, place LN = FD
From N draw the line parallel to DC intersecting Ey at M and NM = Φ it is the **FOOT.**
On Bx, place NQ = FL
From Q draw the line parallel to DC that intersects Ey at P and PQ = Φ^2 it is the **CUBIT.**
In the Middle-Ages these five elements made up the builders' "QUINE".

FIG. 2-10 ~ OTHER REPRESENTATIONS OF THE QUINE

starting from the 1/2 L-shaped square:

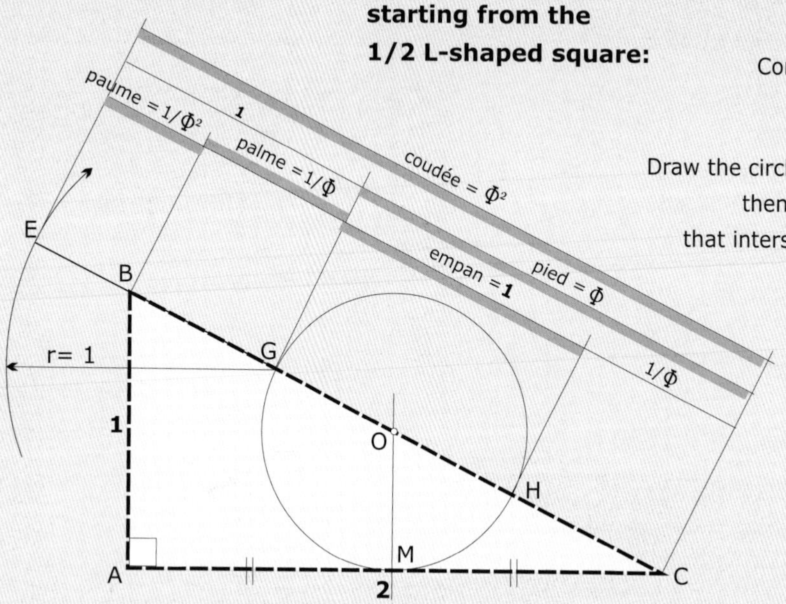

Consider the 1/2 L-shaped square ABC.
MO is the median of AC.

Draw the circle with O as center and OM as radius then from B, draw the arc r = 1 that intersects the prolongation of CB at E.

The figure on the left shows the elements of the Quine.

starting from the golden rectangle:

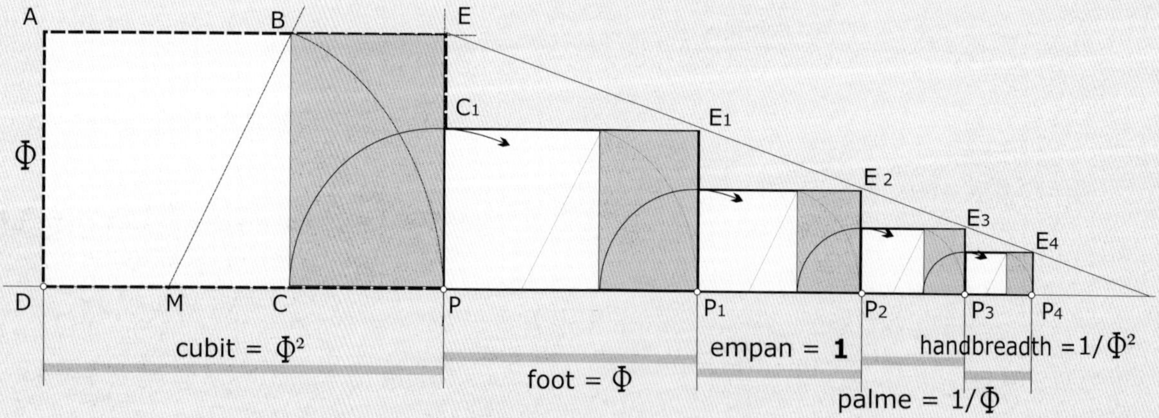

Consider square ABCD with side = Φ and the drawing of the golden rectangle DAEP. It defines the golden rectangle CBEP.

Around P, tip the rectangle CBEP onto C_1, E_1, P_1.
Do the same for P_2, P_3, P_4. The elements of the quine are thus determined.

There are many other ways of finding the values of the quine, see 2-05 page 29 or in the figures of the pentagon (3-11, 3-12) or in the figures of the spirals (4-11 page 66) or (7-10 page 110).
You can have fun finding others.
Those values are the consecutive terms of the FIBONACCI geometric sequence.

FIG. 2-11 ~ THE BUILDERS' OR THE MASTER BUILDERS' STICK

It is only the concrete representation of what was determined with the quine: that length corresponds nowadays to 124.72 cm.

It is composed of five elements and measures 555 lines (one "line" corresponds to 0.224 cm).

This stick refers to human measurements, it is a measuring or a drawing instrument.

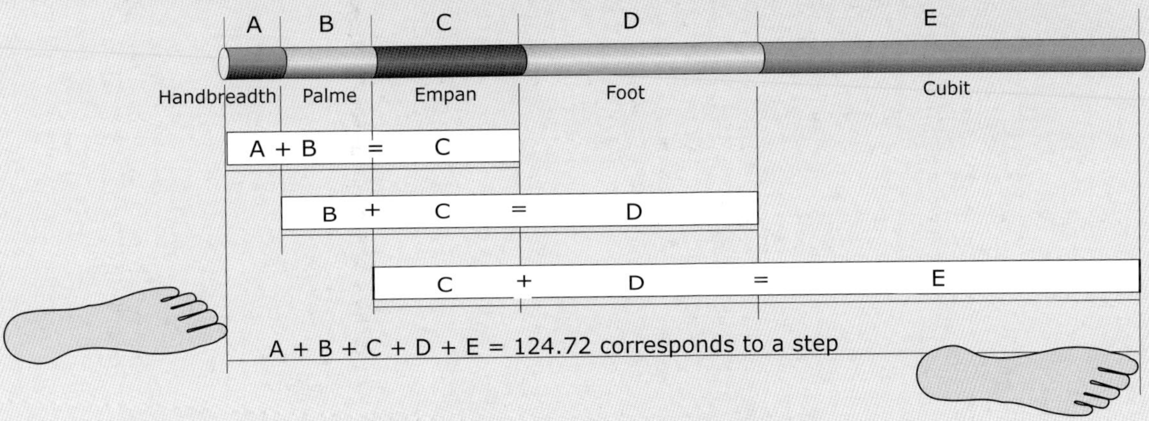

These different measurements follow a double progression:

— a geometric progression of ratio Φ

— a sequence of numbers such as one length = the sum of the two previous ones.

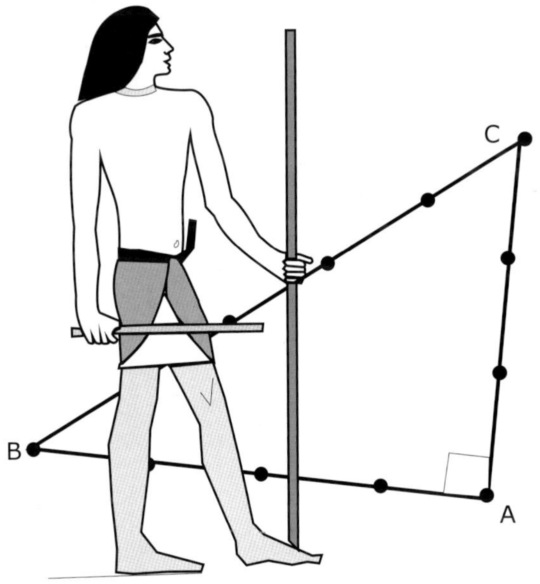

from a drawing by ALLONSIUS.

The measuring and drawing sticks, as well as the knotted rope, already existed in the time of the Egyptian ropestretchers and surveyors.

To survey their fields of alluviums after the Nile's flood, the Egyptians used a rope with knots in 3, 4 and 5 segments that they stretched out to three angles ABC, **the A angle being a right angle**, angle B is about 36° and angle C is about 54°.

36° is the half angle at the vertex of the pentagon: 360° / 5 = 72° = 2 x 36°.

Fig. 2-12 ~ the five articulated arms

measuring instrument of the Romanesque builders

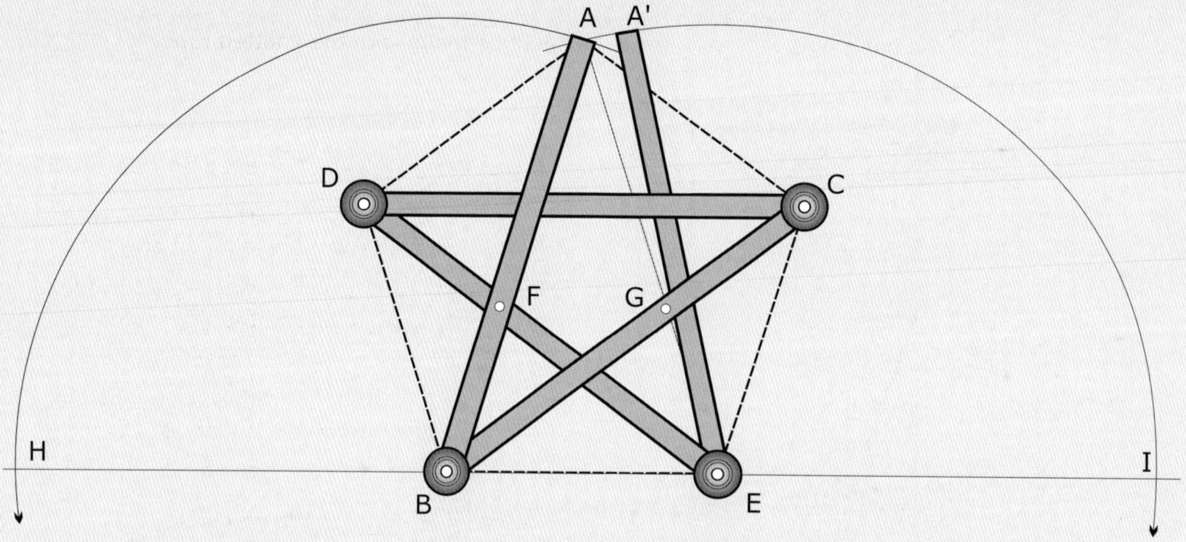

The arms are: AB, BC, CD, DE, EA′ articulated in B, C, D, and E.
Each arm is 20 cm long i. e. = one "empan" = the basic unit.

The 5 arms form a star-shaped pentagon (pentagram) when A and A′ are placed together in A.

FG = 7.64 cm (dimension of the handbreadth = $1 / \Phi^2$)

BE = 12.36 cm (dimension of the palme = $1/\Phi$)

EH = 32.36 cm (dimension of the foot = Φ) obtained by pivoting the BA arm around B and by putting it in line with EB.

HI = 52.36 cm (dimension of the cubit = Φ^2) obtained by pivoting the AB arm around B, the EA′ arm around E and by putting the BH and EI elements on the same line as BE.

we obtain the cubit HI = HB + BE + EI

HI = 20 + 12.36 + 20 = 52.36 cm

$HI = 1 + 1/\Phi + 1 = \Phi^2$.

Fig. 2-13 ~ Basic drawings made with the knotted rope

As well as the five articulated arms, the stick, the surveyors' square, the 1/2 square, ...
the builders had a thin, supple, and not very extensible cord on which they made a knot at every curbit.
The knotted rope could have 10, 12 or 13 knots.

The basic figures of chapter one can all be made with the knotted rope.

examples:

— perpendicular to a straight line, according to Leonardo of Pisa (1220)

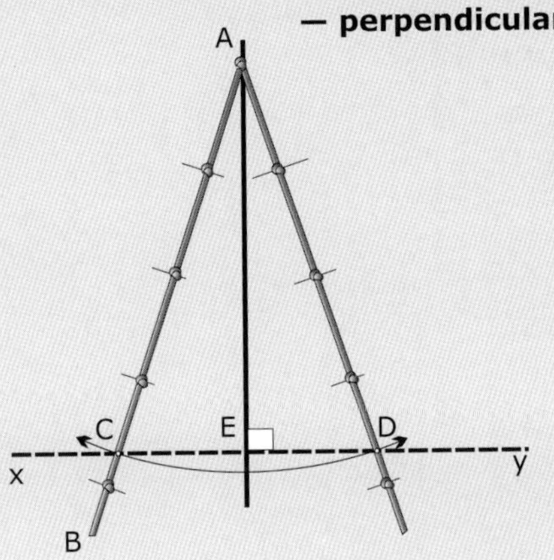

By an A point given on even ground, drop a perpendicular to a straight line already drawn.

At A, fix the extremity of a cord and stretch it so that the other extremity B goes beyond the xy straight line.

Mark point C where the cord meets xy.

With the cord, trace the arc with A for center and AC for radius intersecting xy at point D.

By folding the cord, we obtain E, the middle of CD.

The AE line segment is the perpendicular that was sought for.

— triangle 3-4-5

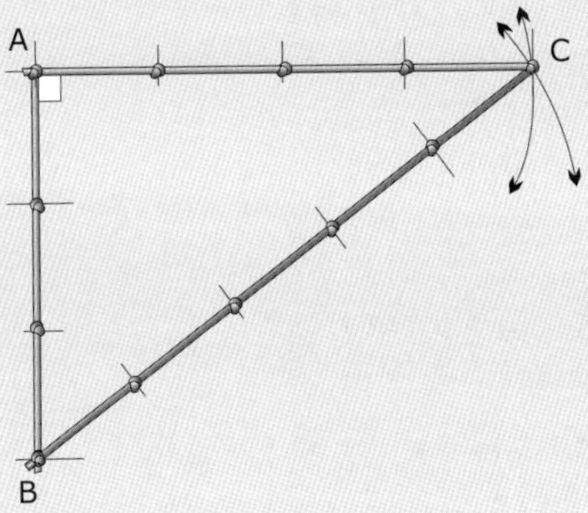

There are other ways to drop the perpendicular to a straight line, with a rope: the most convenient may be that of the 3-4-5 ABC triangle on the left and on page 22, fig 1-10.

— golden rectangle (approximate)

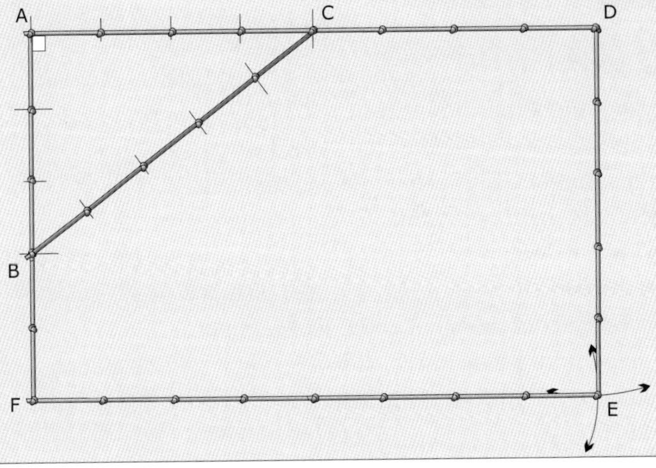

Draw a 3-4-5 ABC triangle and prolong both sides:
AC by 4 cubits onto D
AF by 2 cubits down to F and draw the arcs with D for center then F to obtain E.

The ratio of rectangle ADEF is
AD / AF = 8 / 5 = 16 / 10 = 1.6
which is close to the golden section.

FIG. 2-14 – GOLDEN RECTANGLE BY MEANS OF A KNOTTED ROPE

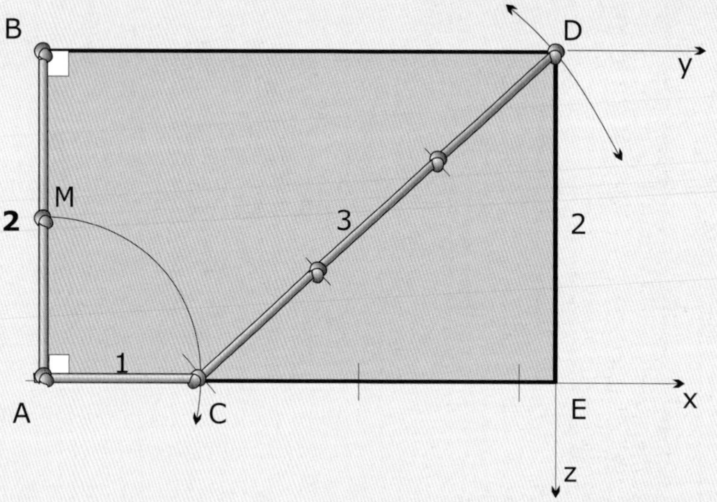

Consider line segment AB = 2 cubits and M the middle of AB.

With the knotted rope:

Draw two half line-segments Ax and By perpendicular to AB at points A and B.
Draw an arc with A as center and a radius equal to a cubit; this arc cuts Ax at point C.
Draw an arc with C as center and a radius equal to 3 cubits. It cuts By at D.
From D, drop a perpendicular (Dz) to By cutting Ax at E.

The ABDE rectangle is a golden rectangle.

Indeed, $Ce^2 = 3^2 - 2^2 = 5$ and $CE = \sqrt{5}$
and $AE = 1 + \sqrt{5}$, hence $AE / AB = (1 + \sqrt{5}) / 2 = 1.618 = \Phi$

That figure shows very well that our ancestral builders were perfectly able to trace all the figures of the present book while being totally ignorant of mathematical formulas and of trigonometry.

Above all, you must not conclude that mathematics are useless, the Pythagoras theorem is there to prove the contrary. Mathematics give the comprehension of the relationships between the parameters and allow to evaluate the approximations obtained by approaching methods.

It is to be noticed that, in all those figures, the real distance between the knots on the cord does not come into account. It must only be the same from one knot to the other... It will be your only obligation if you wish to make such a knotted cord in order to draw beautiful figures on the ground.

In daily life

the pentagon and the dynamics of five

3

FIG. 3-01 ~ BUILDING A REGULAR PENTAGON

Dividing according to mean and extreme ratio an AB line segment, AB representing the diagonal and AM the side AB / AM = Φ

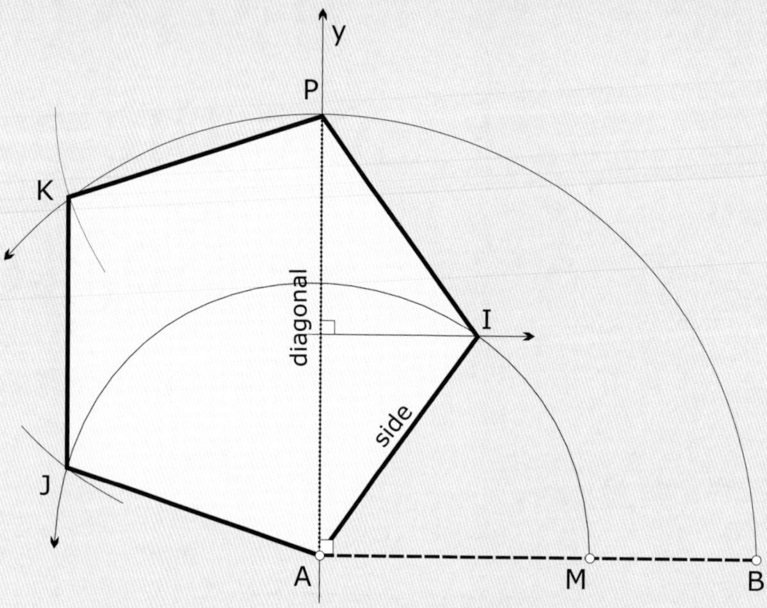

Consider segment AB divided by point M according to mean and extreme ratio (1-11 p. 23).

From A drop the Ay perpendicular to AB.

Draw the arc with A as center and AB as radius that intersects Ay at P.

Draw the median of segment AP.

Draw the arc with A as center and AM as radius that intersects the median of AP at I.

Draw the arc with P as center and PI as radius that intersects the arc with A as center and AB as radius at K.

Draw the arc with K as center and KP as radius that intersects the arc with A as center and AM as radius at J.

The regular pentagon AJKPI has thus been built, clearly showing the relationship between side AI = 1 and diagonal AP = Φ

AP / AI = AB / AM = Φ or more simply: diagonal / side = Φ.

Note: The AB line segment can directly be the diagonal of the regular pentagon, for example KI, which makes the figure easier to build as one only has to trace the sides = AM to obtain P and to trace the diagonals = AB to obtain J and A.

FIG. 3-02 ~ BUILDING A REGULAR PENTAGON

Dividing according to mean and extreme ratio an AB line segment on which the center of the circle circumscribing the pentagon will be built.

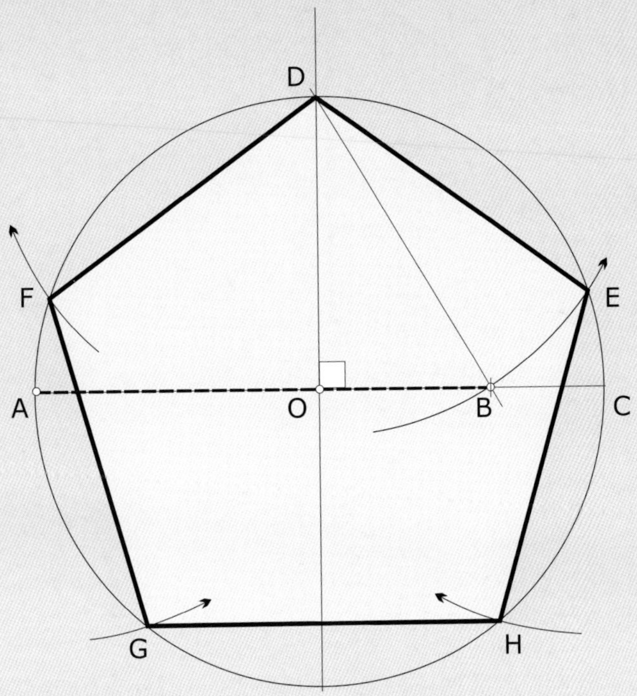

Consider segment AB divided by point O according to mean and extreme ratio (1-11 p. 23).

Draw the circle with O as center and OA as radius. It intersects the prolongation of AB at C.

This circle circumscribes the regular pentagon you want to build.

The perpendicular dropped from O intersects the circle at D DB is the side of the pentagon.

Draw an arc with D as center and DB as radius that intersects the circle with O as center at E and F then from F and E transfer this radius to determine G and H.

The regular pentagon EDFGH has thus been built

$$BD = \sqrt{(3 - \Phi)} = 2.\sin 36°$$

Note: Euclid, a Greek mathematician in the 3rd century B.C., defined the division according to mean and extreme ratio to build a regular pentagon and a decagon more easily.

FIG. 3-03 ~ BUILDING A REGULAR PENTAGON WITH THE 1/2 L-SHAPED SQUARE AND ITS BISECTOR

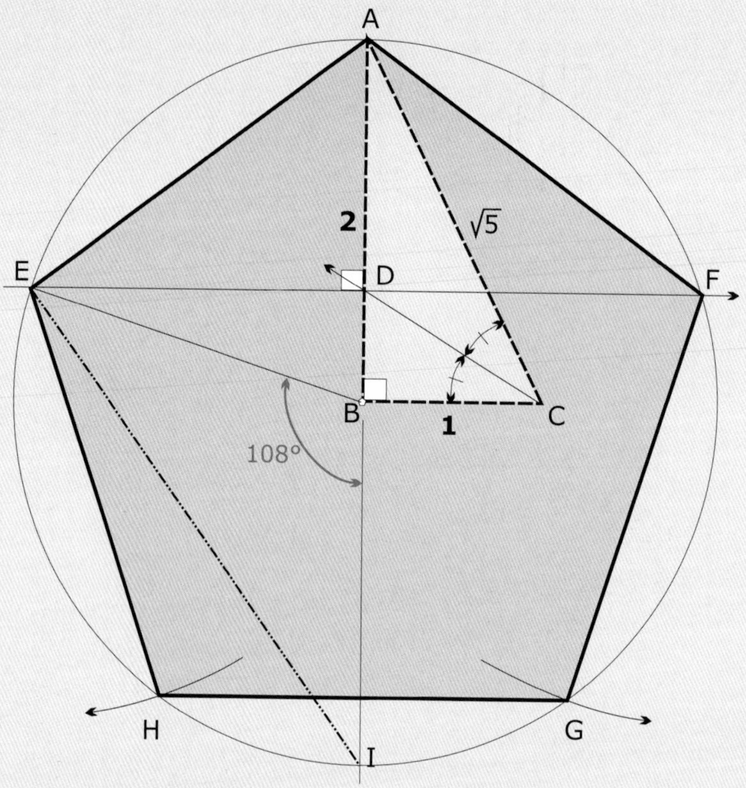

Consider the 1/2 L-shaped square BAC that is right-angled at B, and B the center of the circle with AB as radius that will be the circle circumscribed to the regular pentagon to be built.

Draw the bisector of the ACB angle cutting side AB at D.

By point D, drop the perpendicular to AB cutting the circumscribed circle at G.

Draw the arc with F as center and FA as radius cutting the circumscribed circle at G.

Draw the arc with E as center and EA as radius cutting the circumscribed circle at H.

The regular pentagon AFGHE has thus been built.

Note: A geometric theorem states that in any triangle, the bisector divides the opposite side into segments that are proportional to the adjacent sides.
For the ABC triangle, the opposite side is divided by D in such a way that

$$AD / DB = AC / BC = \sqrt{5 / 1}$$

Line segment EI is called the golden chord. Angle EBI =108°,
it is the angle of a pentagon whose side would be EB and whose
chord would be EI; hence EI / EB = Φ
as here EB = 2, EI = 2 Φ

It is the middle of arc HG, whose chord IG is the side of a regular decagone circumscribed in the circle with A as center and BA as radius.

FIG. 3-04 ~ CONSTRUCTING REGULAR PENTAGONS WITH THE 1/2 L-SHAPED SQUARE

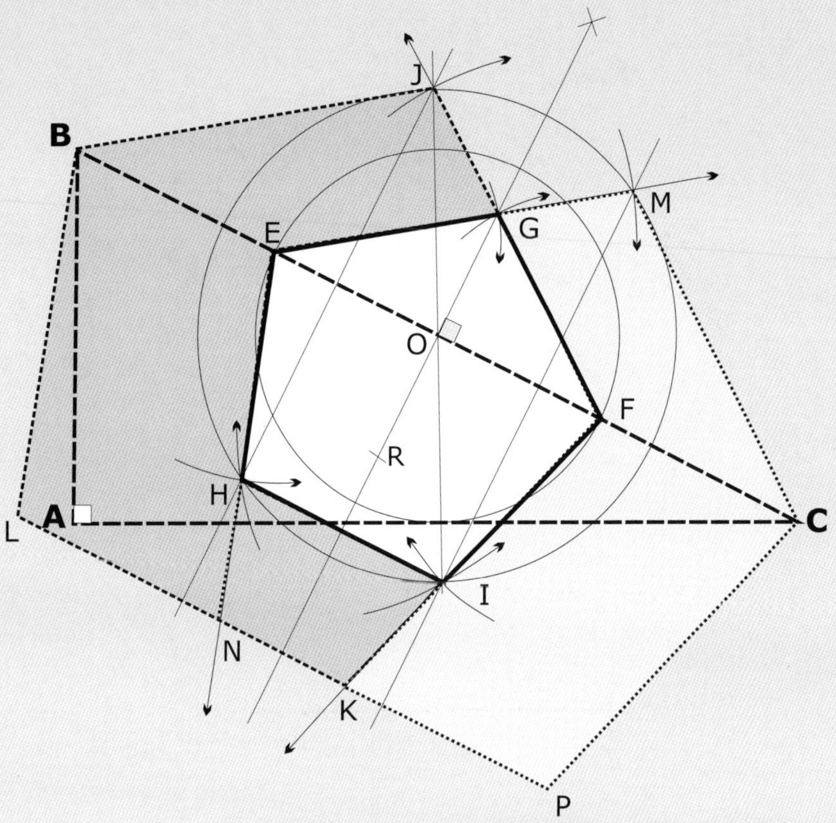

Consider the 1/2 L-shaped square ABC, right-angled at A and O, middle of BC.

Construction of the EGFIH pentagon:

EF / EB = EF / FC = Φ (1-11 page 23)

EF is the diagonal, EB and FC are the sides that will simply be transfered from E and F to define G; transfer EH = EG and FE = FH to define H and I, hence the regular pentagon EGFIH.

Construction of symmetrical regular pentagons:

BF / EF = Φ and symmetrically, EC / EF = Φ

For BJFKL, BF is the diagonal and BJ the side, hence the drawing of that pentagon.

The symmetrical pentagon EMCPN is immediately drawn.

Those two pentagons bear, with the first one EGFIH, a F ratio.

Notes — According to the scale or the position required, we can choose between these three pentagons

— After drawing this figure we can notice:

- that 0I = OJ,
- that JMIH are situated on the same circle with 0 as center
- and above all that, we meet again with the fantastic JIH 1/2 L-shaped square which has a harmonious proportion in relationship to ABC that we started from.

The observation of this figure is a source of new figures to be invented and of other figures included [diamond BJFH ..., pentagon EJMFR (what is to be thought of R ?)... or prolonging BJ, CM,...] It's up to you to continue!

fig. 3-05 ~ constructing a regular pentagon with the 1/2 L-shaped square

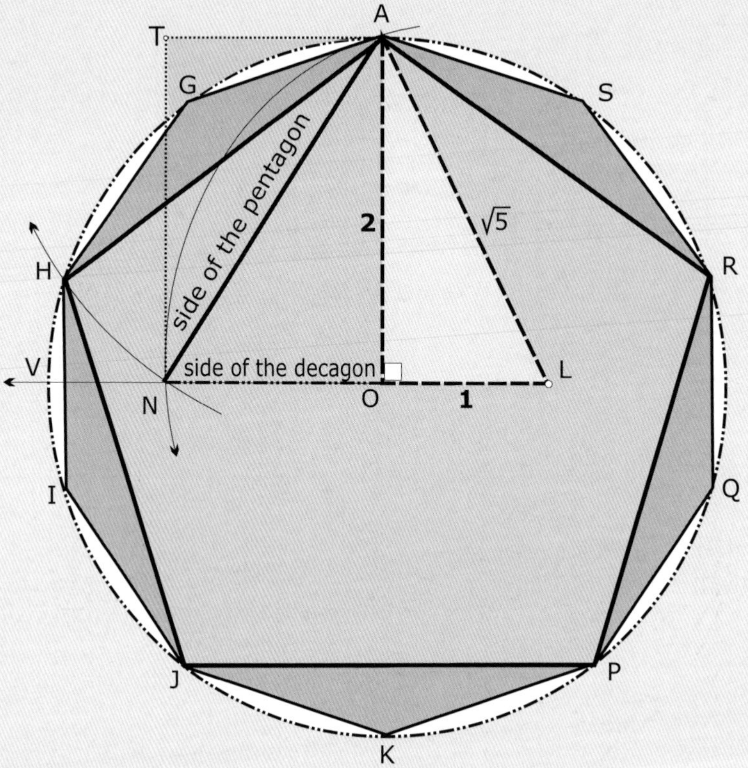

Consider the right triangle OAL (right-angled at O)
It is the 1/2 L-shaped square, OL = 1, OA = 2 and AL = $\sqrt{5}$

Draw the arc with L as center and LA as radius intersecting LO at N.

O is the center of the circle circumscribing the pentagon to be constructed, OA being the radius.

In triangle AON, AN is the side of the pentagon which has only to be transfered from A onto the circumscribed circle to define H and R from where J and P will be defined.

In triangle AON, ON is the side of the regular decagon which has only to be transfered from A to define G and S then from J and P to define the other angles.

The regular pentagon ARPJH is drawn, just as the regular decagon ASRQPKJIHG, from their respective sides: AN and NO.

Notes: — rectangle ONTA is a golden rectangle.
Indeed ON = $\sqrt{5}$ -1 = 2 / Φ therefore OA / ON = Φ.

— Point N could just as well be determined by cutting the OV radius, according to mean and extreme ratio.

fig. 3-06 ~ construction of a regular decagon

with the 1/2 L-shaped square and the golden section

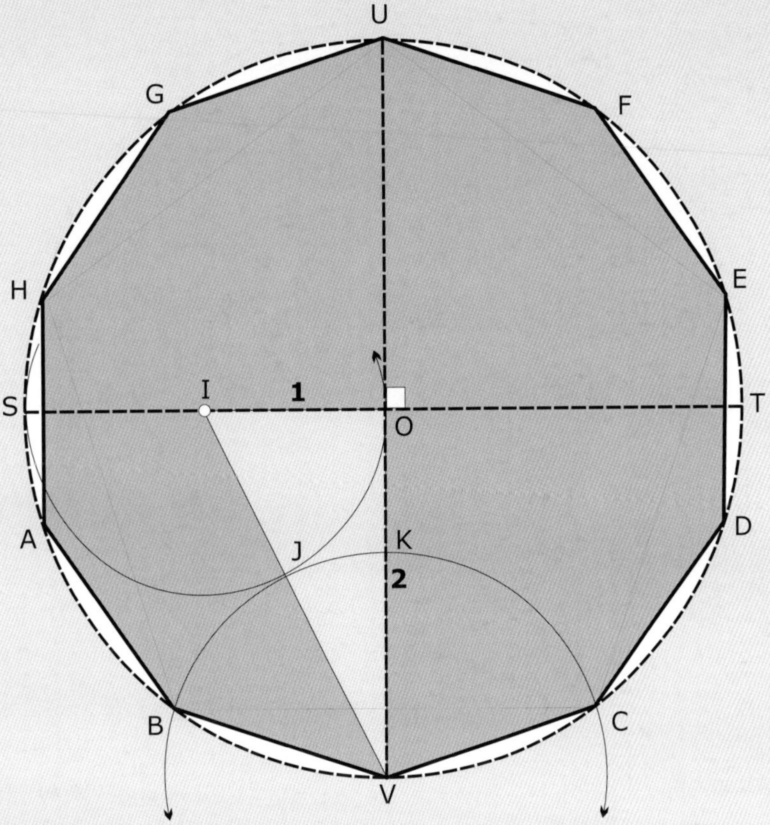

Consider the 1/2 L-shaped square IOV, the circle with O as center and R = 2 as radius and the perpendicular diameters ST and UV (I is the middle of SO).

Draw the semi-circle with I as center and I0 as radius that intersects line segment IV at J.

Draw the arc with V as center and VJ as radius that intersects the O circle at B and C and OV at K.
The CV and BV chords are two sides of the regular decagon.
From C, transfer chords that are equal to BV onto the circle with 0 as center.

You will obtain the regular pentagon VBAHGUFEDC and also directly the BHUEC pentagon.

Note: K divides line segment VO according to mean and extreme ratio
VK / KO = VO / VK = Φ.

FIG. 3-07 – CONSTRUCTING A REGULAR PENTAGON IN A CIRCLE (CHINESE METHOD)

Very interesting and fast method of drawing: approaching method, calculating the approximation.

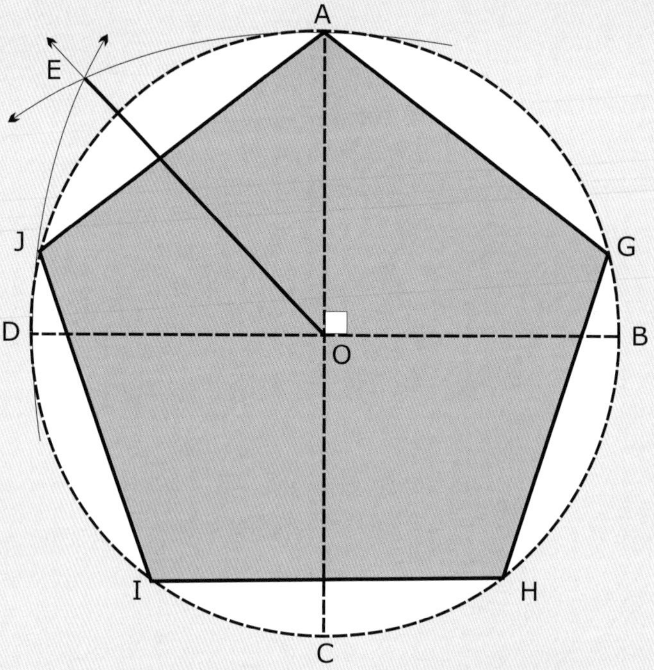

Consider the circle with O as center and the perpendicular diameters AC and BD.

Draw the arc with B as center and BD as radius
then the arc with C as center and CA as radius.

These arcs intersect at E, EO is the side of the regular pentagon.

Transfer the chords that are equal to EO
EO = AG = GH = HI = IJ onto the circle with O as center.
The regular pentagon AGHIJ has thus been built.

As an example, we give here the justification of the drawing method of the Chinese masters where the "c" side is equal to EO and, in the figure, BE = CE = 2R, which amounts to calculating the value of EO in the EBC isosceles triangle**.**

If F is the middle of BC, we get BF = OB sin 45° = EB sin $\widehat{FEB}$
in other words, R sin 45° = 2R sin $\widehat{FEB}$, hence sin $\widehat{FEB}$ = sin 45°/2 = 0.3535
EO = 2R cos $\widehat{FEB}$ - Rcos 45° hence EO / R = 2cos $\widehat{FEB}$ - 0.707 and
EO / R = 1.1637

A precise calculation will give C / R = 1.1755
so, the error is 12 thousandth, which is quite negligible.

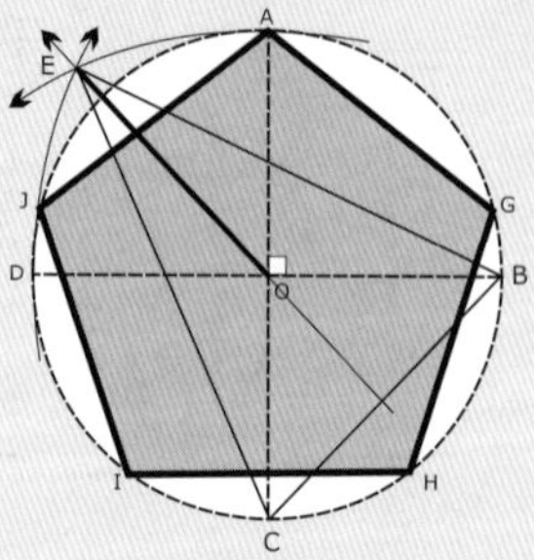

FIG. 3-08 – CONSTRUCTING A REGULAR PENTAGON STARTING FROM A REGULAR HEXAGON,
using only a pair of compasses

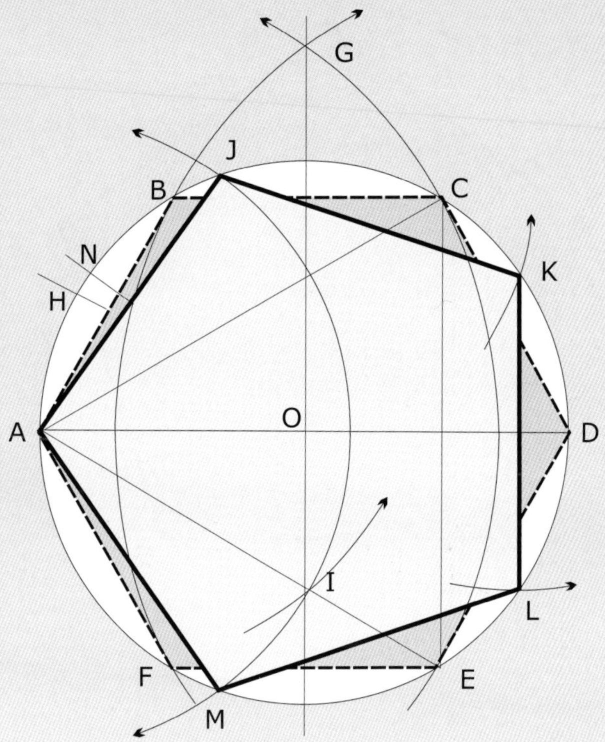

Consider the circle with O as center and OA as radius.

Draw the ABCDEF hexagon, with side OA.

Draw an arc with A as center and AC as radius, then an arc with D as center and DB as radius: these two arcs intersect at G.

Consider H, the middle of arc AB.
Draw an arc with H as center and OG as radius that intersects OG at I.

Draw an arc with A as center and AI as radius that intersects the circle circumscribing the hexagon at J,
AJ is the side of the regular pentagon circumscribed in the circle with O as center.

Thus, you obtain the regular AJKLM pentagon sought for.

Note: 0I is the side of the regular decagon circumscribed in the circle with the 0 center and OA radius: OI = AN = NJ etc...., AD is the symmetry axis of the polygons obtained.

FIG. 3-09 ~ Drawing a regular pentagon starting from the fundamental square

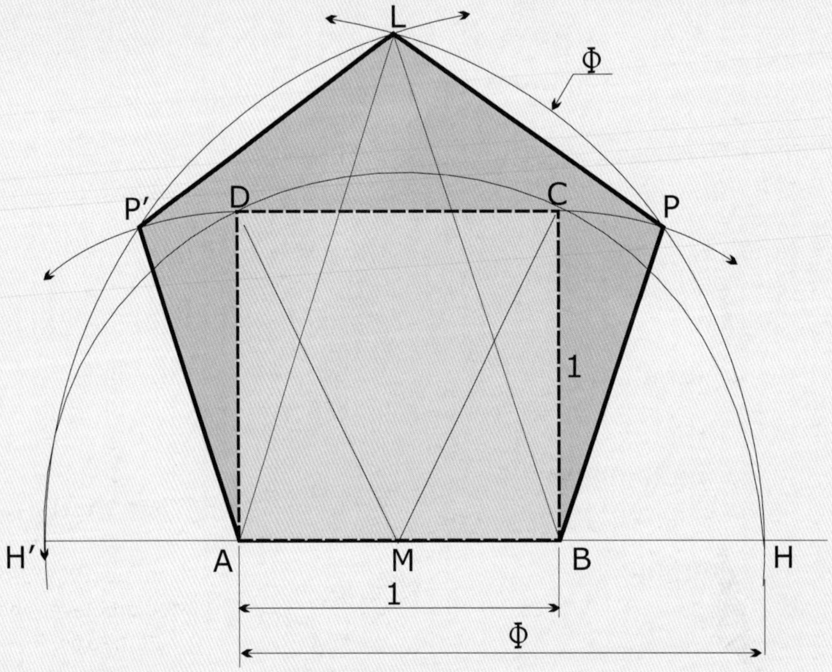

Consider the ADCB fundamental square and M, center of AB.

Draw the arc with M as center and MC as radius that intersects line AB at H and H′.

Draw the arc with A as center and AH as radius, then the arc with B as center and BH′ as radius. These two arcs intersect at L (A, L and B are the angles of the regular pentagon).

Draw the arc with A as center and AD as radius that intersects the arc with B as center and BH′ as radius (already drawn) at P′.

Draw the arc with B as center and BC as radius that intersects the arc with A as center and AH as radius (already drawn) at P.

You obtain the AP′LPB regular pentagon.

fig. 3-10 ~ drawing a pentagram with a knotted rope

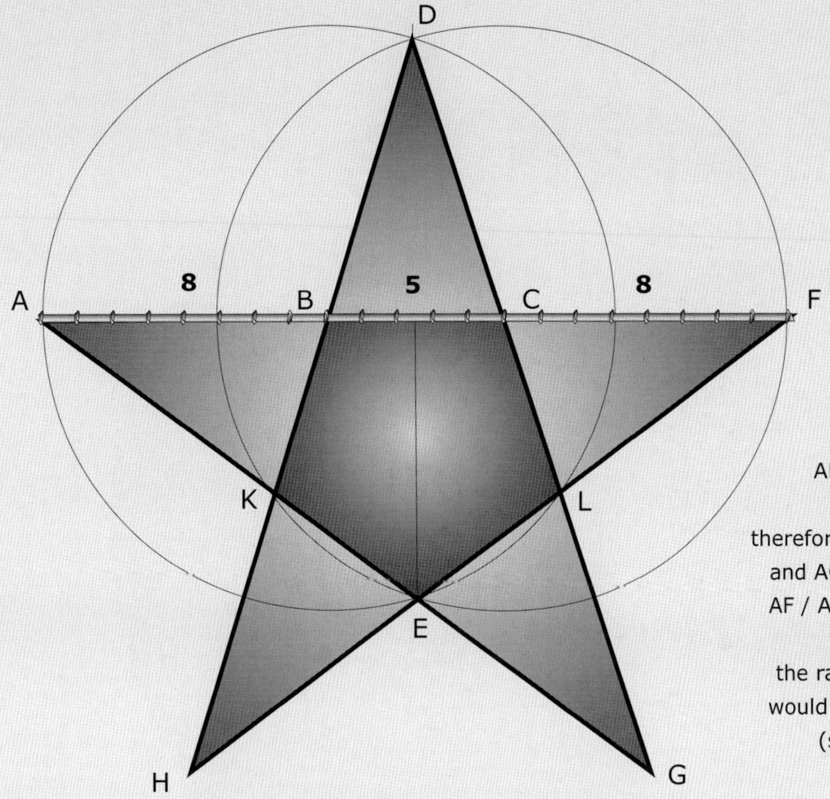

AB = CF = 8 cubits
BC = 5 cubits
therefore, AF = 8 + 5 + 8 = 21
and AC = 8 + 5 = 13 cubits
AF / AC = 21 / 13 = 1.6154

the ratio 55 / 34 = 1.6176
would be even more precise
(see box page 10)

Using a knotted rope, draw a line segment 21 cubits long (AF).
Starting from A, mark point B = 8 cubits and point C = 13 cubits.

Draw a circle with B as center and BA = 8 cubits as radius then a circle with C as center and CF as radius also equal to 8 cubits.
These two circles intersect at D and E.

Straight lines AE and OC intersect at G and straight lines OB and FE intersect at H.
The pentagram has been drawn.

Notes - this figure also determines two inverted pentagons: the BCLEK pentagon and the one obtained by joining AOFGH.

- if the AOFGH pentagram is determined by a nearest ratio ($8 / 5 = 1.6 \approx \Phi$) the figure is visually incorrect; points OBKH cannot be in line to respect the intersections between the circles used to trace the figure and the circle circumscribing the pentagram (see drawing on the right).

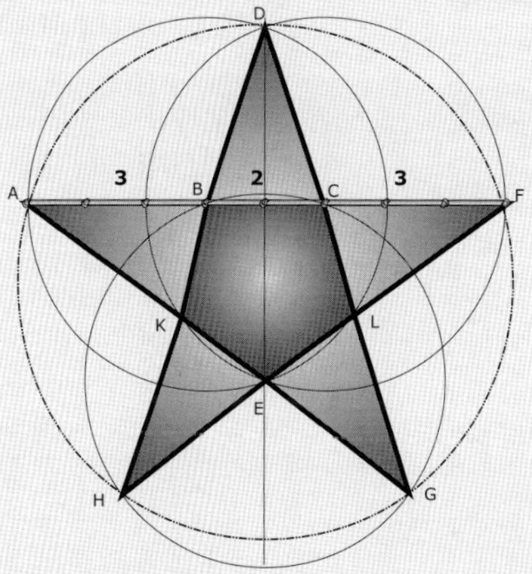

FIG. 3-11 ~ THE REGULAR PENTAGON AND THE "QUINE"

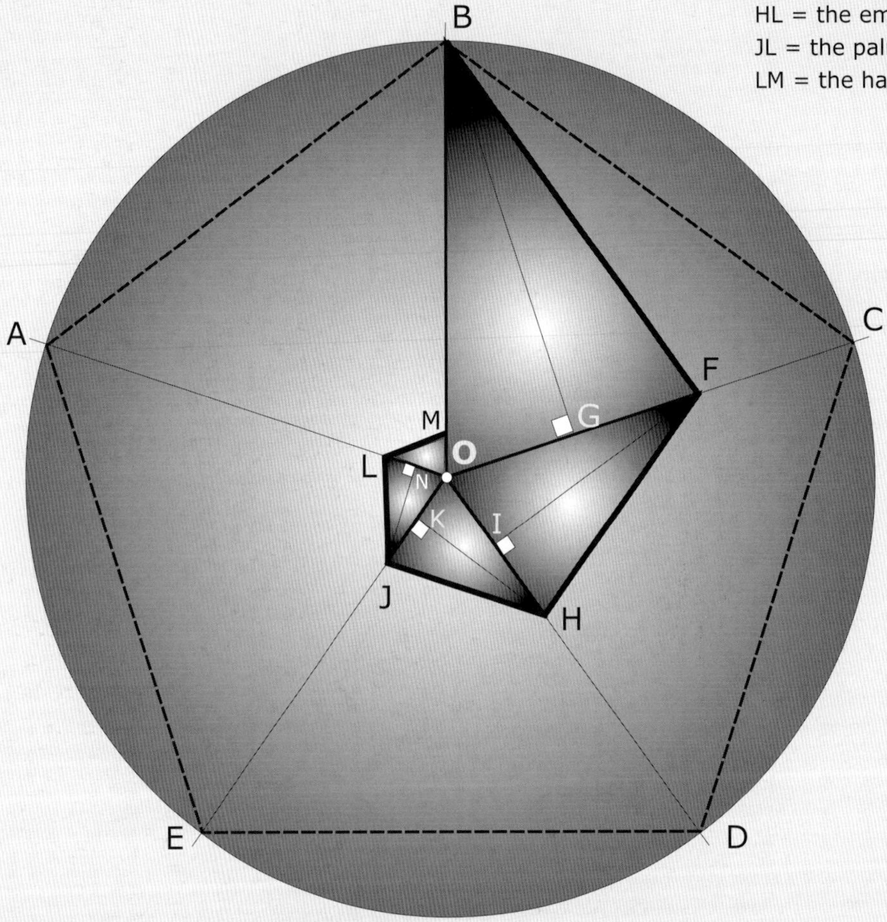

Consider a regular pentagon ABCDF and its five equal radii starting from O, the center of the circumscribed circle.

From B, drop the perpendicular onto OC (point G). On OC, determine OF = 2 OG.

From F draw the same figure, then from H, from J and from L.

You will notice that the AOF, FOH, HOJ, ... triangles, are isosceles triangles with angles of 72° at the base: they are acute golden triangles*.

The segments starting from O: OB, OF, OH, 0J, OL are the five elements of the "quine". The same goes for segments BF, FH, HJ, JL and LM which make up the false spiral BFHJLM.

*an acute triangle is said to be a "golden" triangle when the sides and the base have a Φ ratio.

fig. 3-12 ~ the pentagram and the "quine"

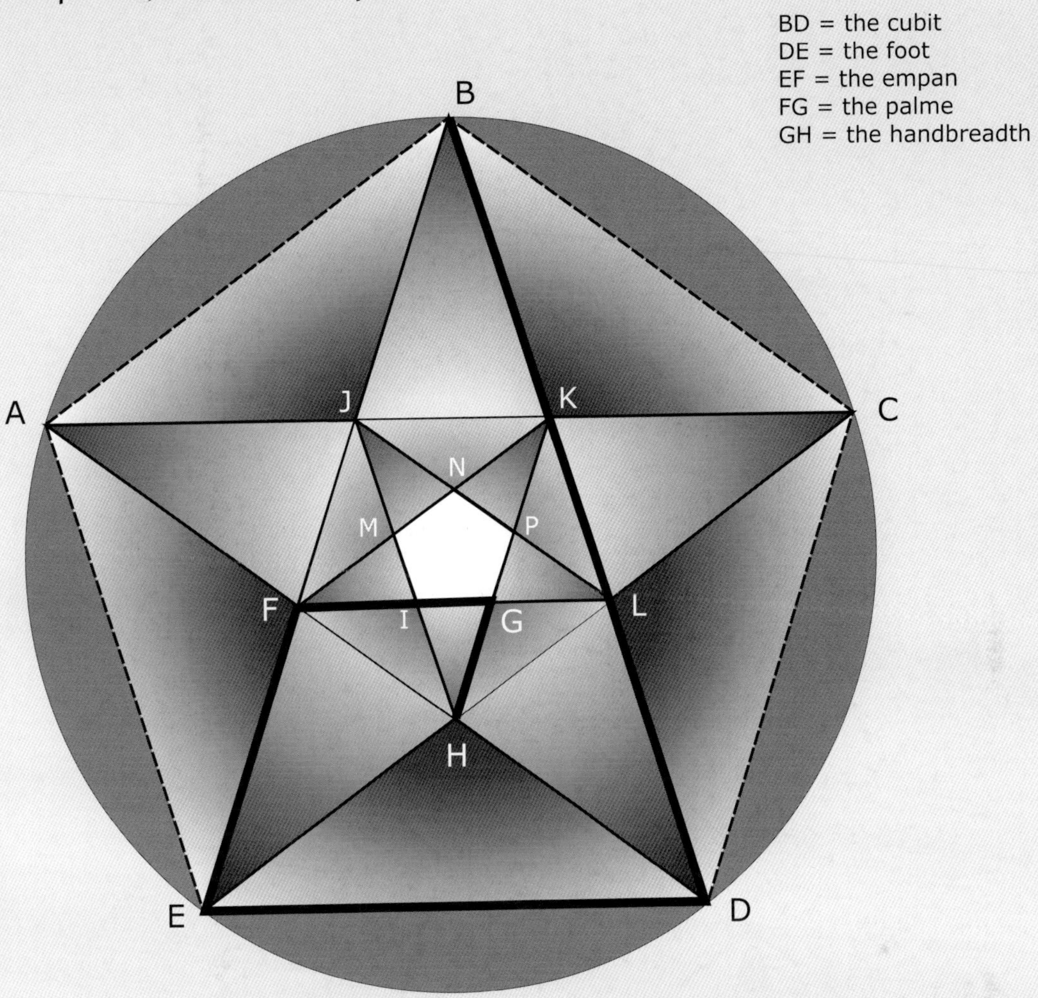

Consider a regular pentagon ABCDE from which the JKLHF and MNPGI pentagrams and pentagons are derived by tracing all the diagonals.

The JKLHF pentagon is inverted and smaller than ABCDE. The same goes for the pentagrams.

The segments of the broken line ADEFGH are the five elements of the "quine", BD being the cubit, DE the foot, EF the empan, FG the palme and GH the handbreadth whose values according to the golden section are indicated on pages 32 to 36.
Here again we find the terms of the Fibonacci series (page 10).

Notes:- other identical polygonal lines can be drawn from A, C, D, or E and form an independent decorative combination.

- draw a pentagram in MNPGI, trace some new broken lines such as ABKPIM, then do the same starting from B, BCLINP, then from C, CDHMPG, etc... new planes come into existence and can be coloured.

FIG. 3-13 ~ ANGLES IN A REGULAR PENTAGON

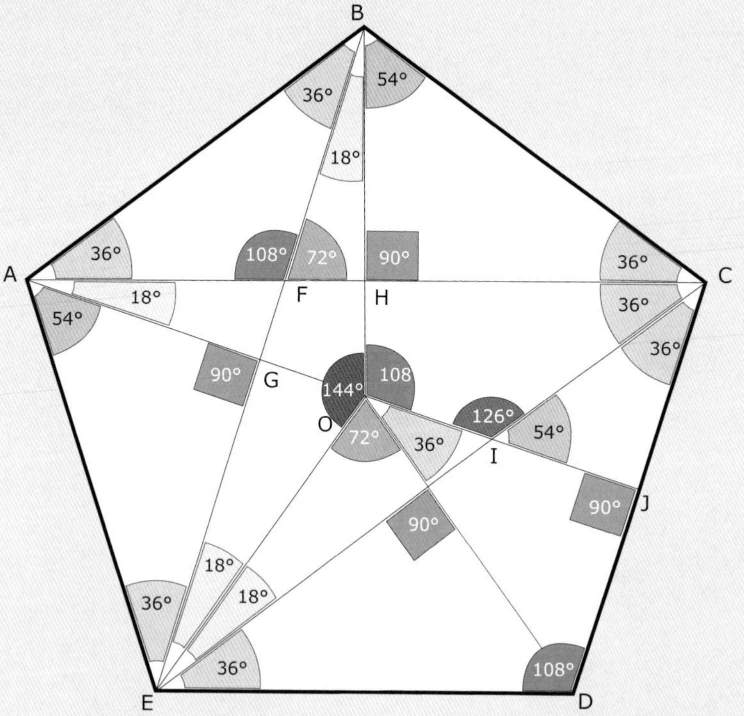

18°
+ 18°
= 36°
+ 18°
= 54°
+ 18°
= 72°
+ 18°
= 90°
+ 18
= 108°
+ 18°
= 126°
+ 18°
= 144°
+ 18°
= 162°
+ 18°
= 180°

The 18°, 36°, 54°, 72°, 90°, 108°, 126°, and 144° angles, are to be found in the regular pentagon. Their arithmetical ratio is 18.

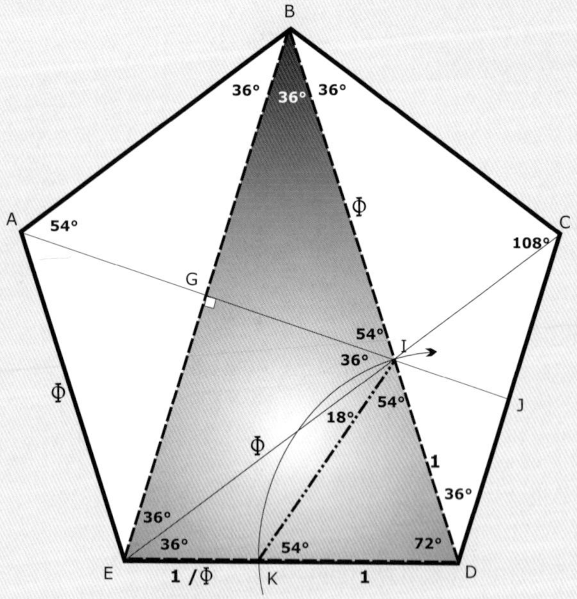

The regular pentagon ABCOE of the figure on the left is composed of two isosceles triangles, ABE = BCD called *"obtuse golden triangles"* or **divine triangles*** (4-04) and of an isosceles triangle EBD called *"acute golden triangle"* *or* **sublime triangle*** (4-06)

AJ is the median of BE and OC. It is the height of the pentagon.

CE is one of the diagonals of the pentagon, So are BE or BD.

The figure shows the angles and the values according to the golden section.

Note: if AB = 1, CE = BE = BD = Φ

* lyrical name given in European Middle Ages.

Fig. 3-14 ~ Angles of a regular decagon

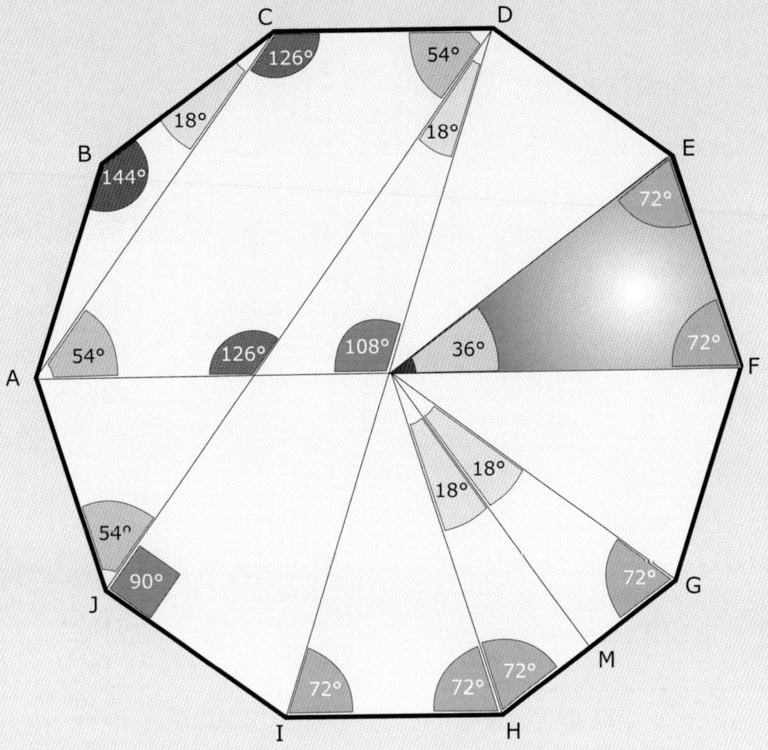

As in the pentagon, one can find 18°, 36°, 54°, *72°*, 90°, 108°, 126°, and 144° angles.

Fig. 3-15 ~ Drawing 36° 72° 108° angles with the 1/2 L-shaped square

dividing according to mean and extreme ratio (1-11 page 23).

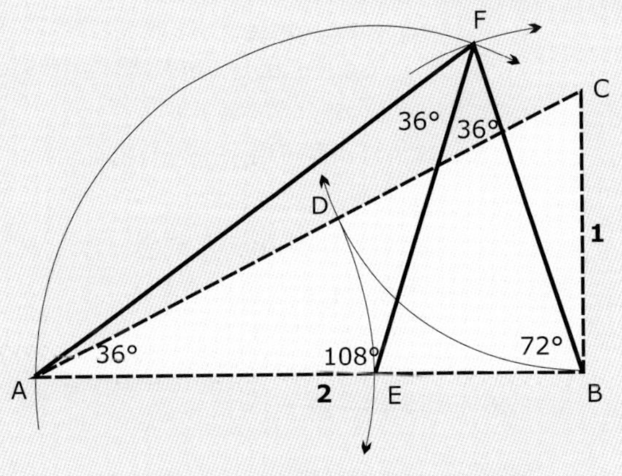

FE is the bisector of angle AFB

Consider the 1/2 L-shaped square ABC And its parting into AB / AE = Φ.

Draw the arc with E as center and EA as radius then the arc with B as center and EA as radius; these arcs intersect at F.

The AFE (obtuse) and EFB (acute) triangles are again to be found with their characteristic angles (see at the bottom of this page on the left).

SPECIAL PAGE, ...

for the readers wishing to determine with mathematical precision the approximations in the figures drawn by approaching methods or for the inquisitive readers who want to discover the demonstrations justifying the figures we propose.

A few useful values

	$\Phi^5 = 11.090$
	$\Phi^4 = 6.8535$
	$\Phi^3 = 4.2358$
	$\Phi^2 = 2.6180$
$\sqrt{\Phi} = 1.2720$	$\Phi = 1.618034$
$\sqrt{5} = 2.236068$	$1 = 1$
$\pi = 22 / 7$	$1 / \Phi = 0.6180$
$\pi = 1.2\ \Phi^2$	$1 / \Phi^2 = 0.3820$
$\pi = 4 / \sqrt{\Phi}$	$1 / \Phi^3 = 0.2361$
π = 6 coudées	$1 / \Phi^4 = 0.1459$
$\pi = 3.141593$	$1 / \Phi^5 = 0.0902$

Trigonometric values, according to Φ, of the principal angles that have been encoutered in the figures proposed.

Angles	Sinus	cosinus	tangente
18°	$1/ (2\ \Phi) = 0.309$	$\sqrt{2+\Phi}\ / 2 = 0.951$	$1 / ((1+\Phi)\sqrt{3-\Phi}) = 0.325$
26.56° (half L-shqped square)	$\Phi / (\Phi+2) = 0.447$	$2\ \Phi / (\Phi+2) = 0.894$ (sinus x 2)	$1 / 2 = 0.500$
36°	$(1 / 2).\sqrt{3-\Phi} = 0.587$	$\Phi / 2 = 0.809$	$\sqrt{3-\Phi}\ / \Phi = 0.726$
51.83° (chéops)	$\sqrt{\Phi} / \Phi = 0.786$	$1/\Phi = 0.618$	$\sqrt{\Phi} = 1.272$
53.13° (3-4-5)	$4 / 5 = 0.800$	$3 / 5 = 0.600$	$4 / 3 = 1.333$
54°	$\Phi /2 = 0.809$ (cosinus 36°)	$(1 / 2).\sqrt{3-\Phi} = 0.587$ (sinus 36°)	$\Phi / \sqrt{3-\Phi} = 1.377$
72°	$\sqrt{2+\Phi}\ / 2 = 0.951$ (cosinus 18°)	$1/ (2\ \Phi) = 0.309$ (sinus 18°)	$(1+\Phi) . \sqrt{3-\Phi} = 3.077$

Note: the angle 26.56° (1/2 L-shaped square) is equal to the half angle 53.13° (triangle 3-4-5)

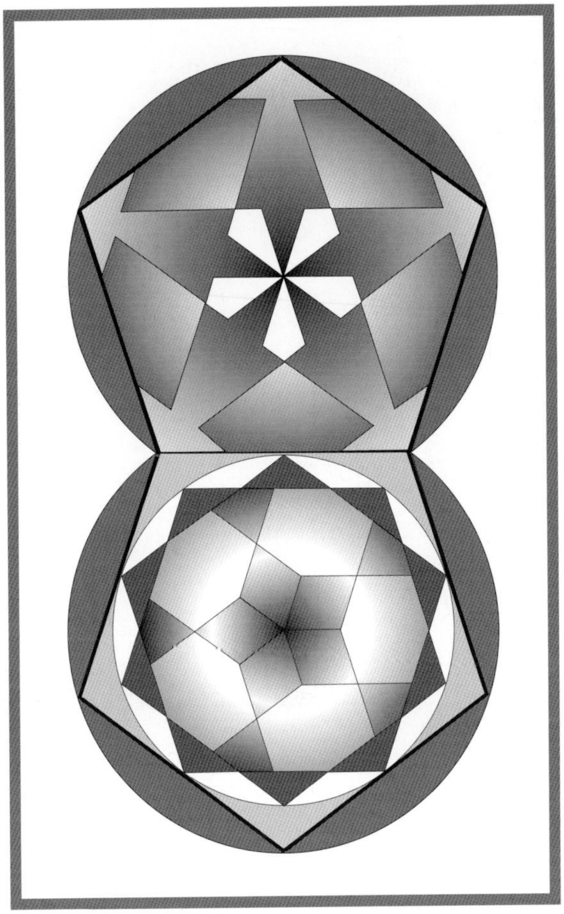

Creativity

Figures where Φ can be found

4

Fig. 4-01 ~ Silver rectangle in which Φ can be found

obtained by dividing any segment according to mean and extreme ratio.

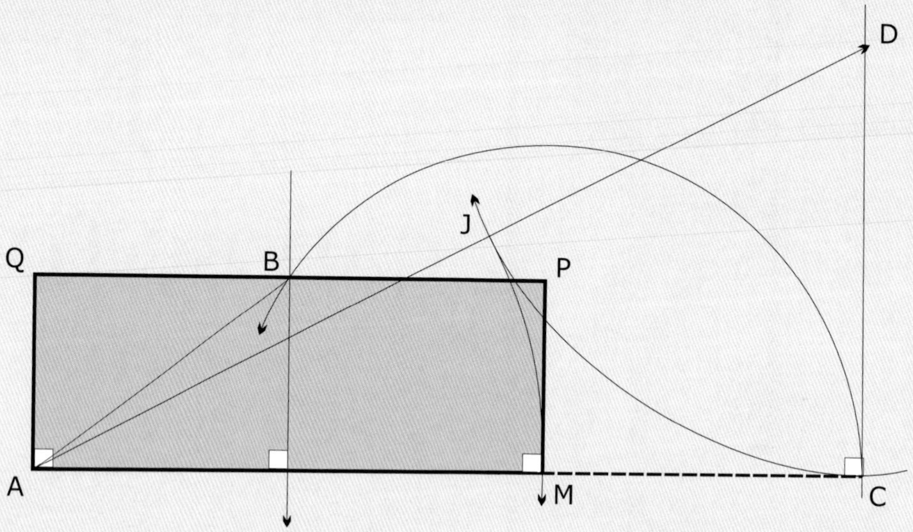

Consider line segment AC.
Divide segment AC according to mean and extreme ratio (1-11 p 23)
M divides AC according to mean and extreme ratio.

$AM / MC = AC / AM = \Phi$.

Trace the median of AM.

Draw the arc with M as center and MC as radius cutting the median of AM at B.

From M and A, drop the perpendiculars to AM.

From B, trace a parallel to AC that intersects
the perpendiculars starting from A and M at Q and P.

You obtain the "silver rectangle" AQPM.

The ratio of its sides being: $K = AM / MP = 2\,\Phi / \sqrt{(3-\Phi)}$.

Note: we name "silver rectangle" any rectangle in which the
ratio of the sides can be expressed according to Φ.

fig. 4-02 ~ silver rectangles where Φ, 1/Φ, 1/Φ² and the golden rectangle can be found

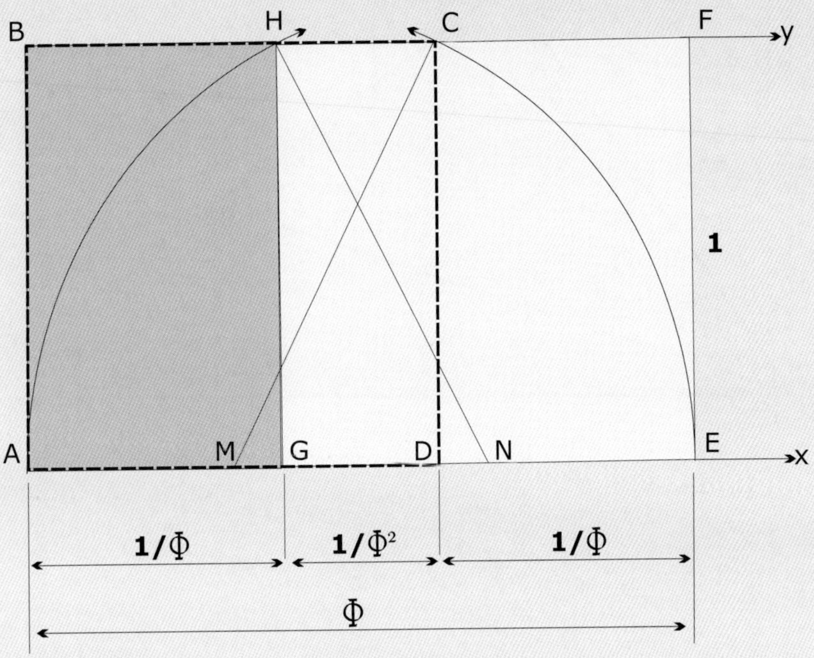

Consider the ABCD fundamental square with 1 for side and M as middle of AD.

Build the golden rectangle ABFE (2-01 page 26).

Build a second fundamental square EGHF along EF, N being the middle of GE.

The ABFE and ABHG rectangles are golden rectangles. The ratio of the sides is $K = \Phi$

The GHCD rectangle is a silver rectangle The ratio of the sides is $K = \Phi^2$

Note: It is possible to draw other golden rectangles starting from the dlvision according to mean and extreme ratio or from the fundamental square (see figure to the right) but also from the 1/2 L-shaped square, from the pentagon,...

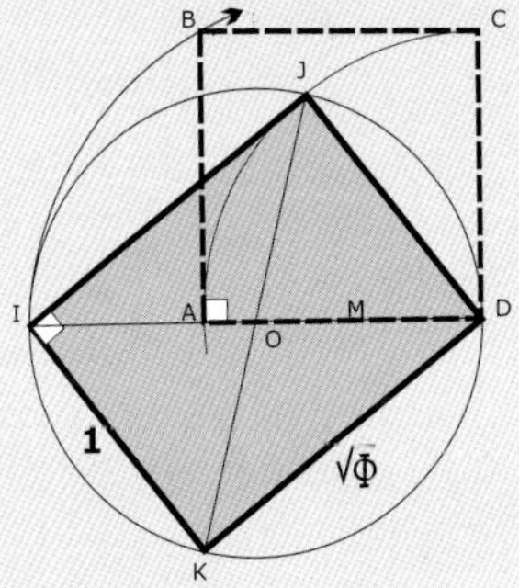

FIG. 4-03 ~ THE RIGHT TRIANGLES WHERE Φ CAN BE FOUND

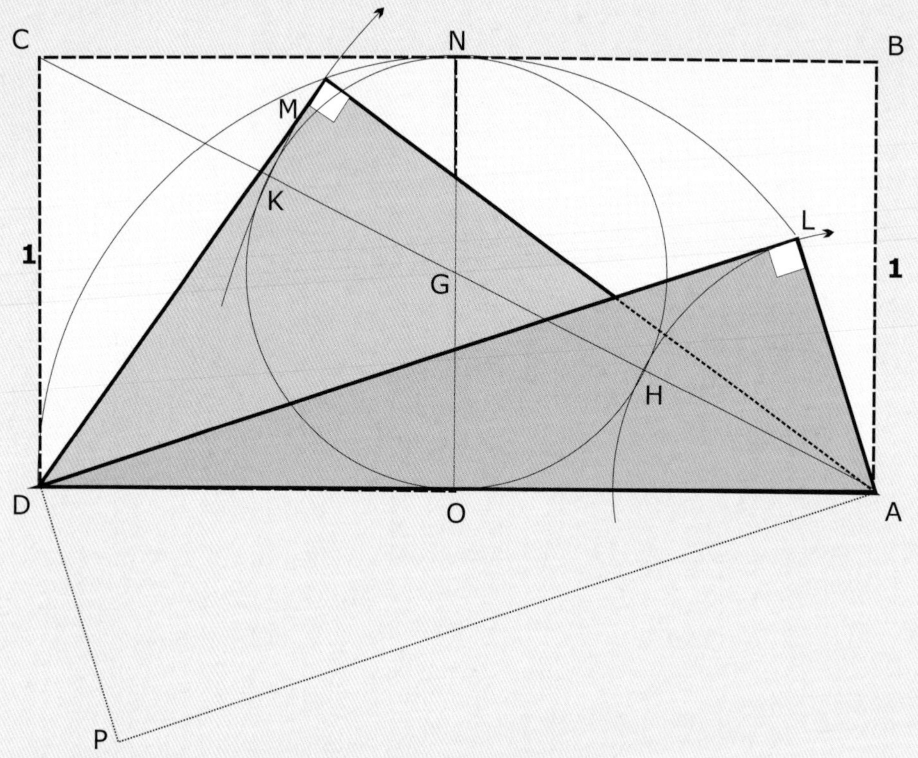

Consider the double square ABCD with CD = 1, O and N being the middle of AD and BC.
Draw line segment AC.

Draw the circle with G as center (middle of ON) and with a GO radius that intersects AC at K and H
KH / AH = KA / KH = Φ hence : KA = Φ.

Draw the semi-circle with O as center and DA as diameter
(it is tangential to line segment BC at N)

Draw the arc with A as center, with AH as radius
intersecting at L the semi-circle with O as center.

The right triangle DLA is right-angled at L
hypotenuse AD = 2 side AL = 1/Φ and LD = $\sqrt{(\Phi+2)}$

Draw the arc with A as center and with AK as radius
intersecting at M the semi-circle with O as center.
You obtain the right triangle DMA that is right-angled at M
hypotenuse AD = 2 side MD = $\sqrt{(3 - \Phi)}$ and AM = Φ

Notes: - this figure also makes it possible to define the silver rectangles, for example: DLAP.
- this figure could just as well start from the 1/2 L-shaped square or from the Barlong rectangle.

fig. 4-04 ~ the triangle where Φ can be found, called the "divine" triangle

(obtuse triangle)

Consider the golden rectangle AEFD (2-01 page 26).

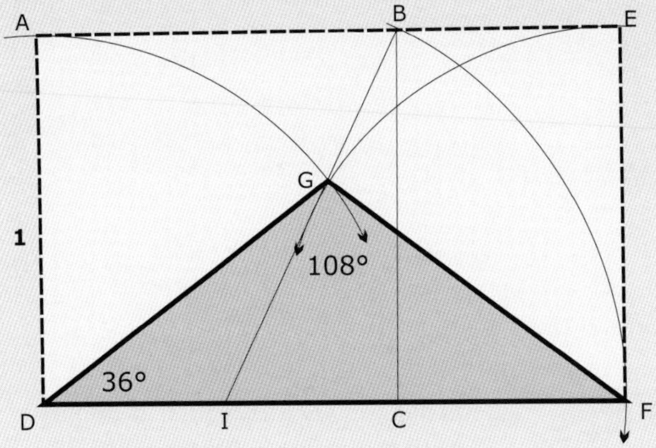

Draw the arc with F as center and FE as radius, then, draw the arc with D as center and DA as radius: these two arcs intersect at G.

In this isosceles triangle DGF (called "divine triangle") the basis is Φ,the sides = 1 and the height $0.5 \times \sqrt{(3 - \Phi)}$

It is to be noted that angles GDF and GFD = 36° and angle DGF = 108°.
It is a part of a pentagon with its diagonal.

fig. 4-05 ~ the triangle where Φ can be found with the regular pentagon

Consider the regular pentagon ABCDE with side = 1 (3-02 page 41).

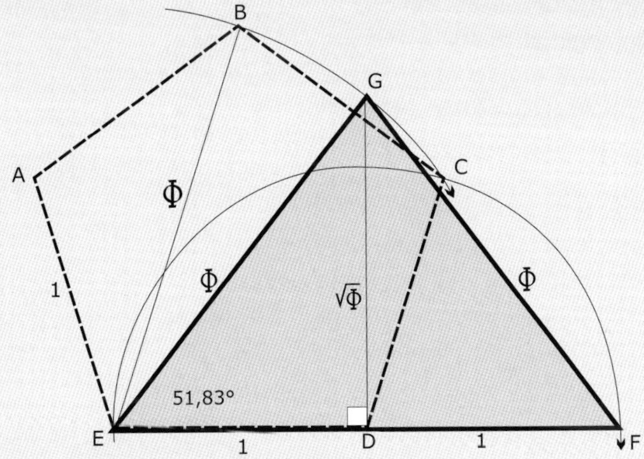

Draw the semi-circle with D as center and DE as radius intersecting ED at F.

Draw the median of segment EF.

Draw the arc with E as center and EB as radius intersecting the median of segment EF at G.

The isosceles triangle EGF has a base = 2, sides = Φ and height = $\sqrt{\Phi}$.

Note: the GEF angle corresponds to the angle of the apothem of the Cheops pyramid.

FIG. 4-06 ~ THE TRIANGLE WHERE Φ CAN BE FOUND, THE "SUBLIME" TRIANGLE

The sublime (acute) triangle with the regular pentagon.

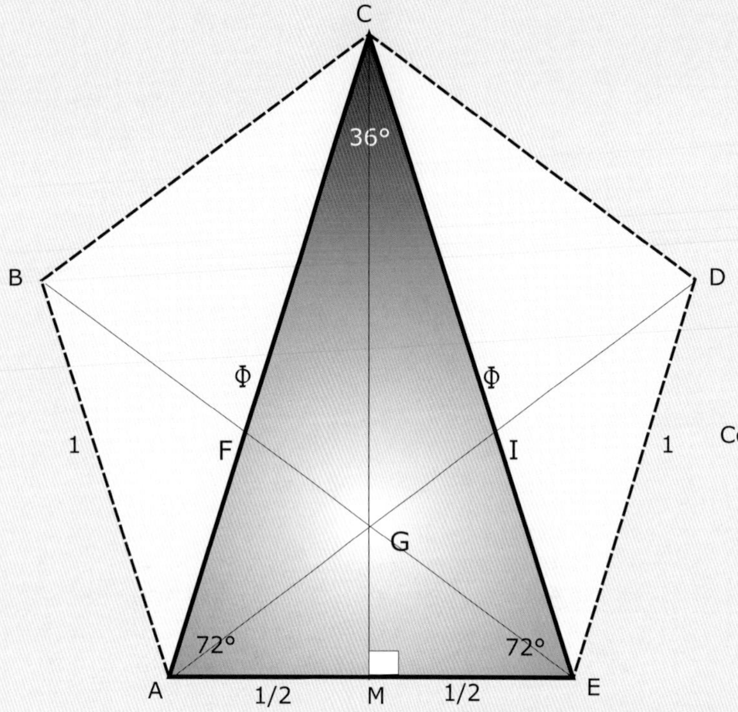

Consider the ABCDE regular triangle with the ratio (3=01 page 40) diagonal / side = Φ.

Draw diagonals CA and CE. From C, draw the height CM of the pentagon.

The isosceles triangle ACE has thus been determined, called the "sublime triangle". Its characteristics are:

— the angles at the base (72°) are worth twice the angle at the vertex (36°)

— AC/AE = Φ, in other words, if its base = 1, its sides = Φ

— value of the height MC = $0.5 \times \sqrt{(3+4\,\Phi)} = 1.538$ this height is also the bisector of the angle at the vertex

— the bisector EF of an angle at the base, for example angle E, (that is also a diagonal of the pentagon) determines in the triangle a new sublime triangle AFE with FE / FA = Φ.

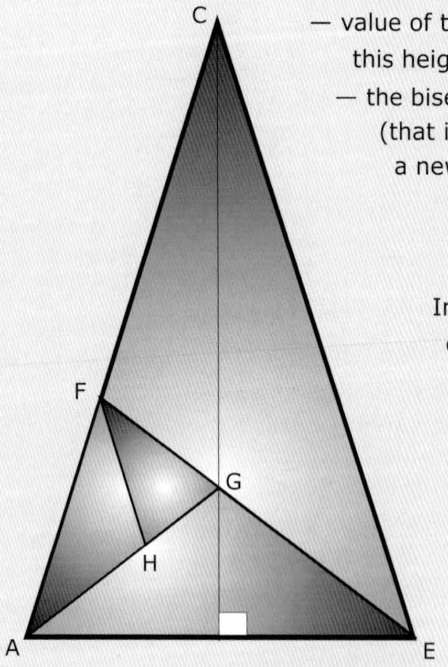

In the new triangle AFE, the bisector of A determines the AFG angle then, in this triangle (also a sublime triangle) the bisector of F determines another sublime triangle FGH and so on...

Hence, the figure on the left in which you will also notice:

ACE is composed of sublime and divine triangles

— If CE = a cubit, EA = a foot, AF = 1 empan FG = a palme and GH = 1 handbreadth (Fibonacci p.10) it is possible to establish the elements of the relation.

FIG. 4-07~ SPIRAL IN A PENTAGON BY MEANS OF SUBLIME (ACUTE) TRIANGLES

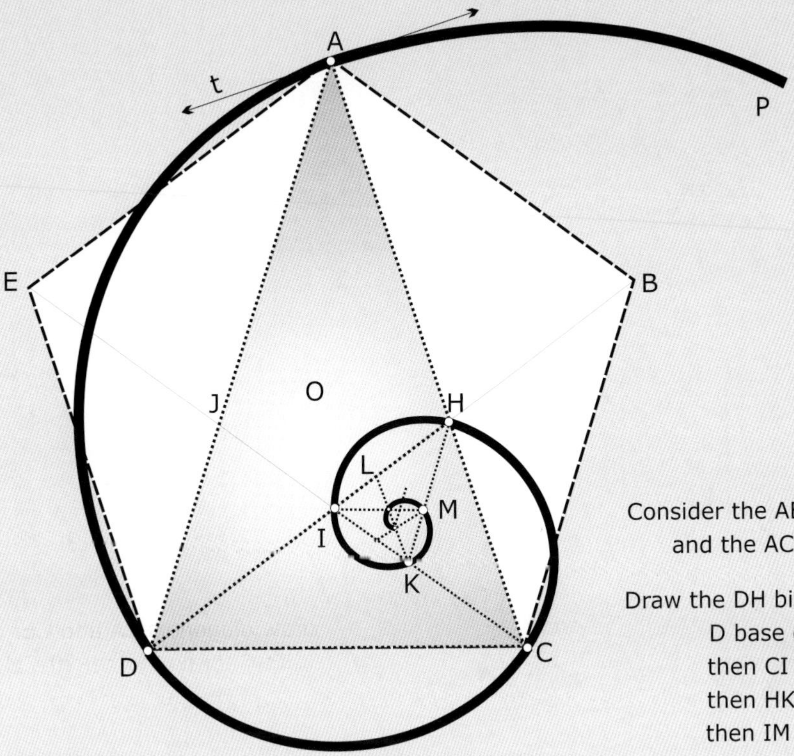

Consider the ABCDE regular pentagon and the ACD sublime triangle.

Draw the DH bisector of angle D at the D base of triangle ACD, then CI of triangle CDA, then HK of triangle HCI, then IM of triangle IHK, ...

Draw the spiral following the conditions of tangency allowing the arcs to be correctly linked:

- at A, the arc with C as center and CA as radius for arc AP and the arc with H as center (on AC) and HO as radius for arc AD.
- at O, the arc with H as center and HO as radius for arc DA and the arc with I as center (on HD) and ID as radius for arc DC.
- the same goes for C, H, I, K, M, etc.

The PADCHIKM ... spiral has thus been drawn.

Notes: — in triangle CDH: AC / CO = Φ or CD = DH
hence CA / HD = HD / IC = IC / KH = ... = Φ.
Two consecutive arcs of the spiral have a Φ ratio like the terms of the Fibonacci sequences.
— by symmetry to the vertical axis you can obtain the figure on the right and a symmetry to the horizontal axis would make it possible to obtaln 4 spirals.
— see note page 63 (4-09).
Here, for A: the centers are H and C, for D, I and H...

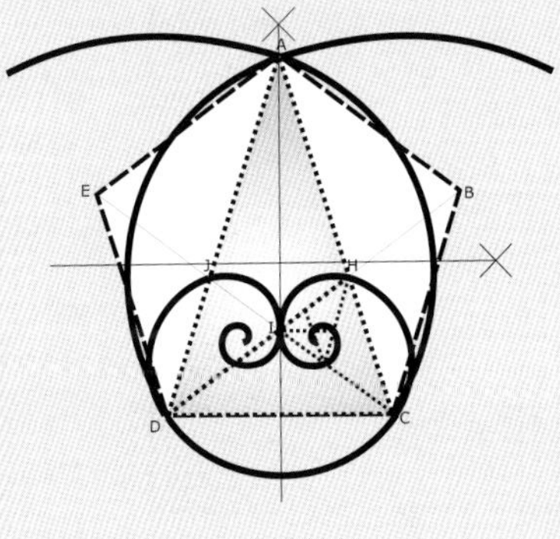

Fig. 4-08 ~ Golden spiral by means of regular pentagons

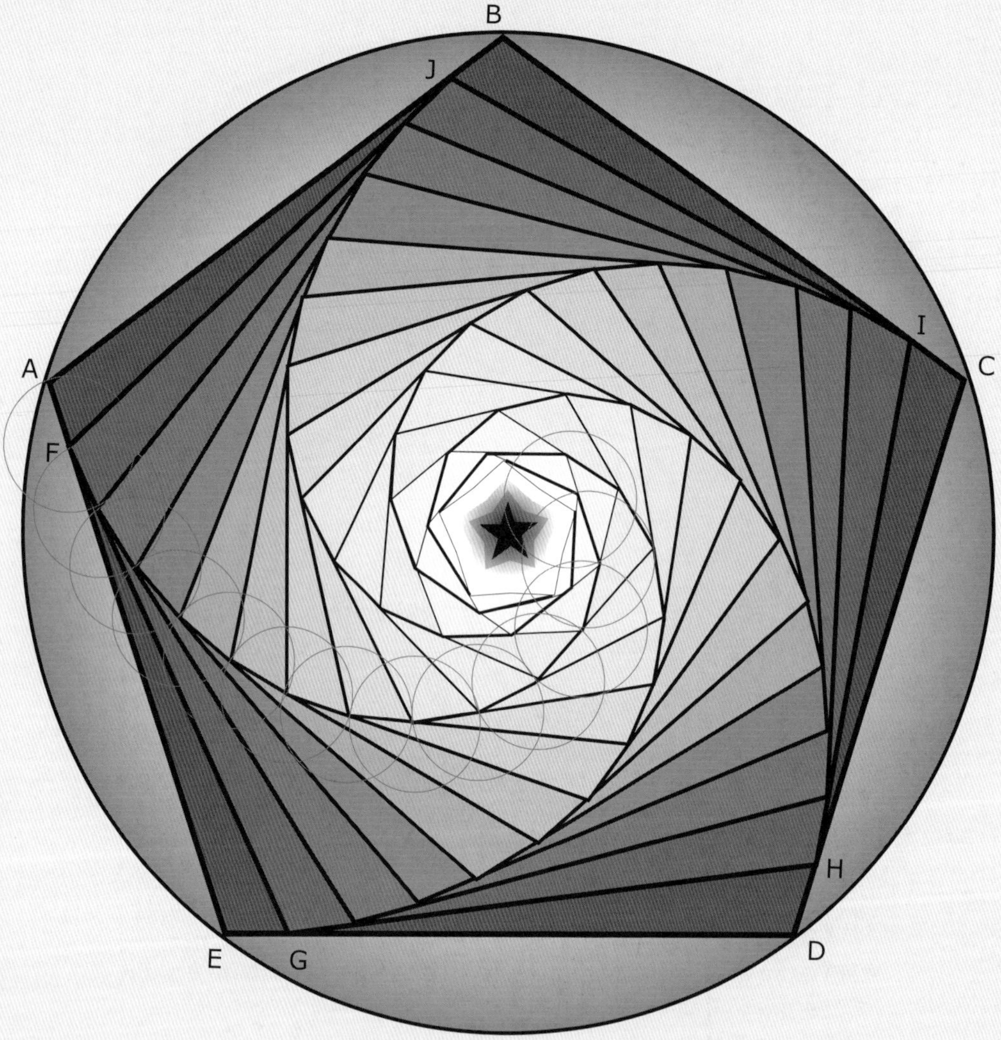

Draw the ABCDE regular pentagon (3-01 page 40).

On AE delimit a chosen length AF = 1.

To place this length you trace a succession of circles as shown on the figure.

On ED delimit EG = 1, on DC delimit DH = 1.

On CB delimit CI = 1, on BA delimit BJ = 1.

You will obtain the FJIHG regular pentagon.

Continue tracing other regular pentagons that get smaller and smaller.

In the center, draw a pentagram.

Fig. 4-09 ~ the golden spiral by means of golden rectangles

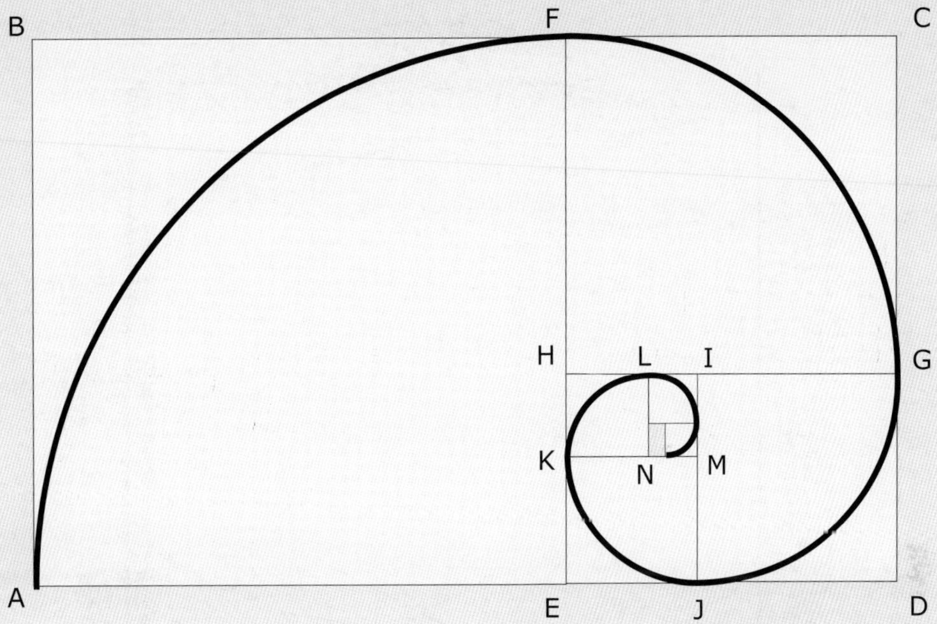

Consider the first golden rectangle ABCD and square ABFE (2-01 page 26).

Draw the arc with E as center and EA as radius (arc AF).
Draw a second golden rectangle FCDE and square FCGH.
Draw the arc with H as center and HF as radius (arc FG).
Draw a third golden rectangle GDEH and square GDJI.
Draw the arc with I as center and IJ as radius (arc GJ).
Draw a fourth golden rectangle JEHI and square JEKM.

Draw the arc with M as center and MK as radius (arc JK).

Do the same for arc KL, and the following others.

Thus, we obtain the AFGJKL golden spiral....

Notes: — It is a "false spiral" because it is composed of arcs instead of having a continuous variation in radius.

— the connections between the arcs are always perfect because the condition of tangency is respected (1-12 page 24) example: F being the common tangent, centers E and H are on the same straight line perpendicular to the tangent.

fig. 4-10a ~ double spiral on a heptagon

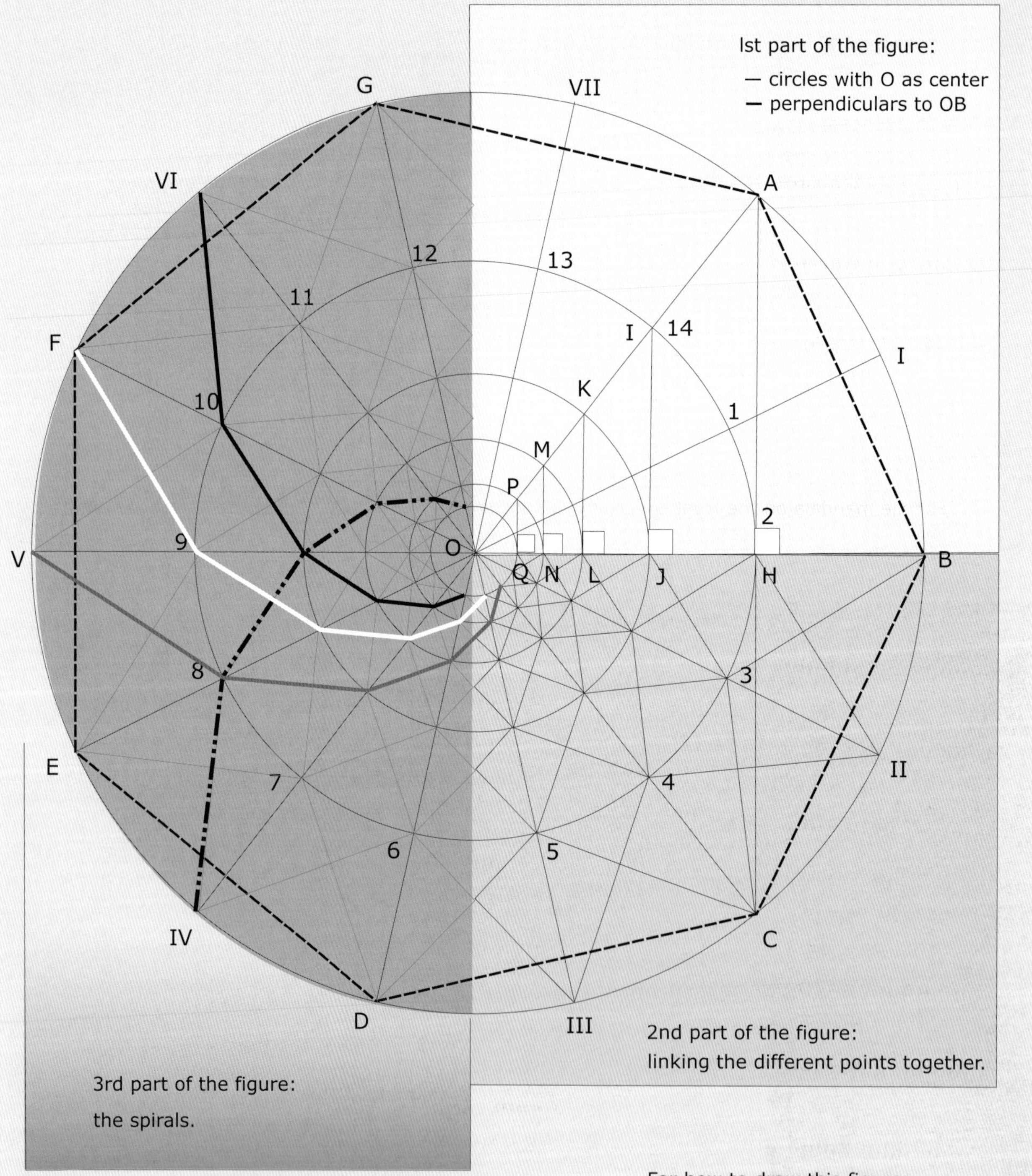

For how to draw this figure:
see on the next page.

FIG. 4-10B ~ DOUBLE SPIRAL ON A HEPTAGON

Text corresponding to figure 4-10a on the previous page.

Consider the ABCDEFG regular heptagon (for how to draw it, see 7-12 page 113) and O the center of the circumscribed circle.

Ist PART: draw the AC arc that intersects radius OB at H and separates OB according to mean and extreme ratio (1-11 page 23) then draw the circle with OH as radius.
From this new circle with OH as radius, draw IJ which produces the circle with OL as radius and so on till you get to the smallest radius you have chosen (these radii bear a Φ ratio).

2nd PART: determine the middle of arcs AB, BC... so as to obtain points I to VII then, draw the "network" by joining together each circle and each radius (1-2, 2-3), for example B to 3, II to H...

3rd PART: (on the left of the vertical axis) join the points, according to the example, to obtain the spirals represented by a continuous line or the second spirals shown by a dash-dotted line.

Note: This figure is possible for a heptagon because 360°/ 7 is close to the 51.8° angle necessary to obtain the similar triangles bearing a Φ ratio.
For the mandala on the front cover of this book starting from a pentagon, the drawing is different.

Cones in spirals and
spirals on each cone:
thus Nature has a little fun
with the romanesco cabbage

and, strangely enough,
by their shape and their number,
those spirals bear a relationship
to the golden section.

Fig. 4-11 ~ Golden rectangle divided by 1/2 L-shape squares having sides = 2 the builders' "quine"

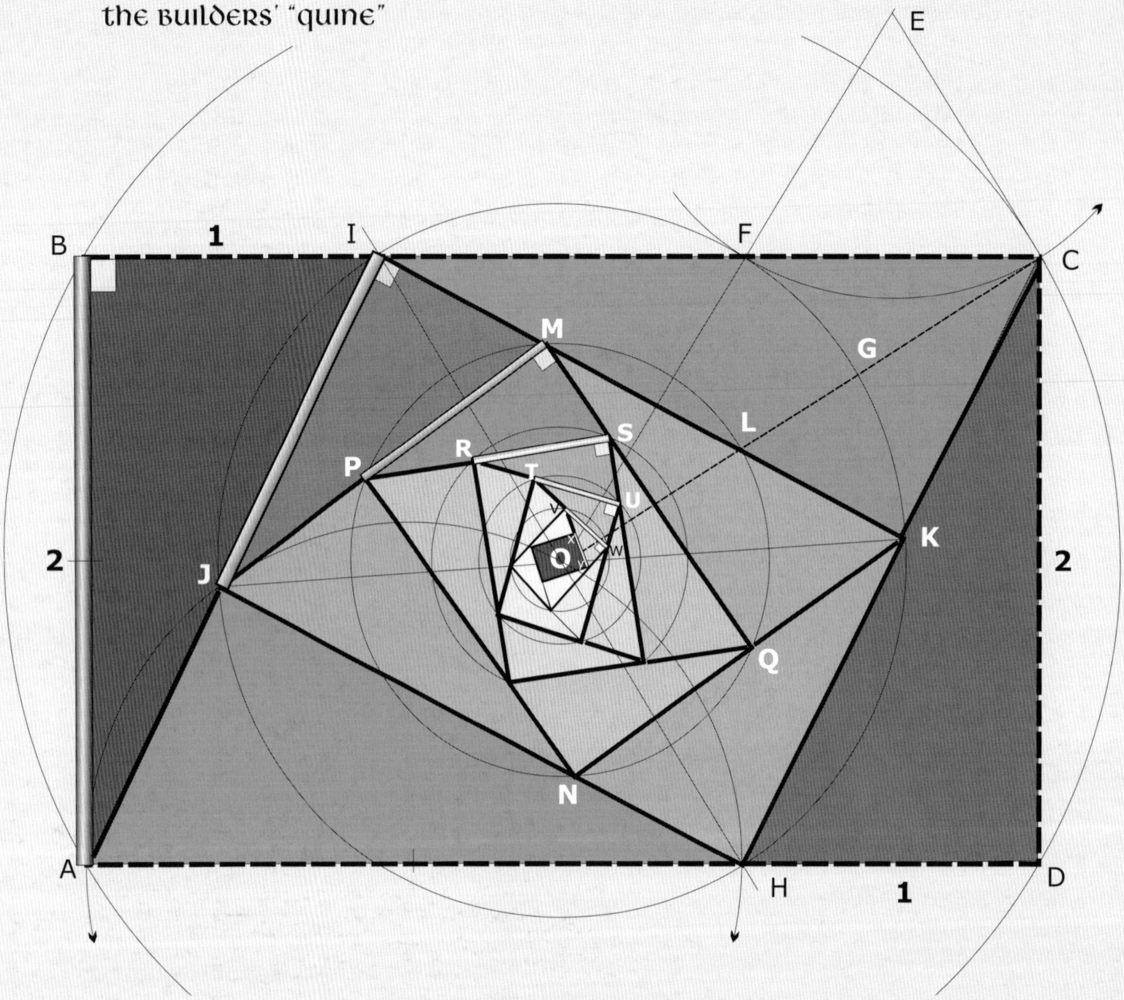

Consider the golden rectangle ABCD with O as center of the circumscribed circle.
Divide OC according to mean and extreme ratio.

OG / GC = OC / OG = Φ.

The circle with O as center and OG as radius intersects AD at H and BC at I.
The semi-circle with AH as diameter intersects the circle with OG as radius at K.

Four equal right triangles have thus been built
ABI, ICK, CDH, AJH.

Divide OG according to mean and extreme ratio, OL / LG = OG / OL = Φ.
As previously, determine points M, N, P, Q, and so on
till you have drawn the 6 x 4 = 24 triangles of this figure.
The concentrical circles have radii in the Φ proportion.
AB is the **cubit**, JI the **foot**, PM the **empan**, RS the **palme**
and TU the **handbreadth**.

(Imagine the broken lines BIMSUWY ... or AJPRTVX ... that can be drawn and coloured)

FIG. 4-12a ~ Golden rectangle divided by 1/2 L-shaped squares and the dextrorotatory swastika

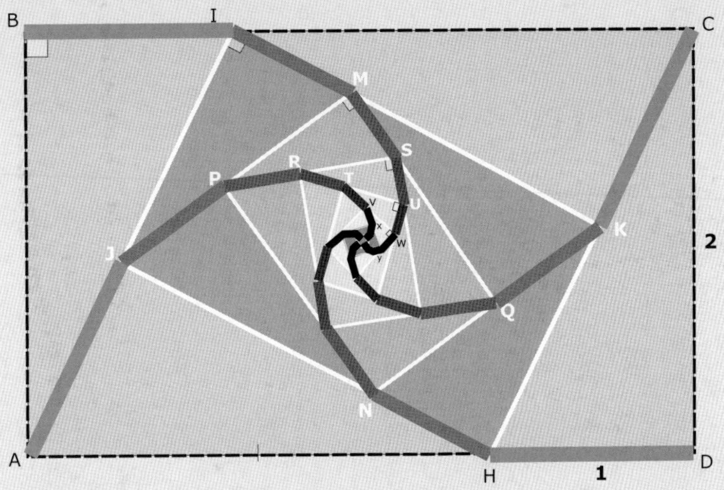

The golden rectangle with the 1/2 L-shaped squares of the previous figure makes it possible to draw 4 broken lines starting from A, B, C, D, representing the Hindu religious symbol the **dextrorotatory Swastika** (turning to the right) that means Peace.

The swastika of sinister memory had arms turning to the other direction.

For each of those lines the ratio of two consecutive segments is always equal to **Φ.**

For example: BI / IM = Φ, i.e. the ratio of the progression of the length of the segments (see page 10).

FIG. 4-12b ~ Golden rectangle divided into diamonds by 1/2 L-shaped squares

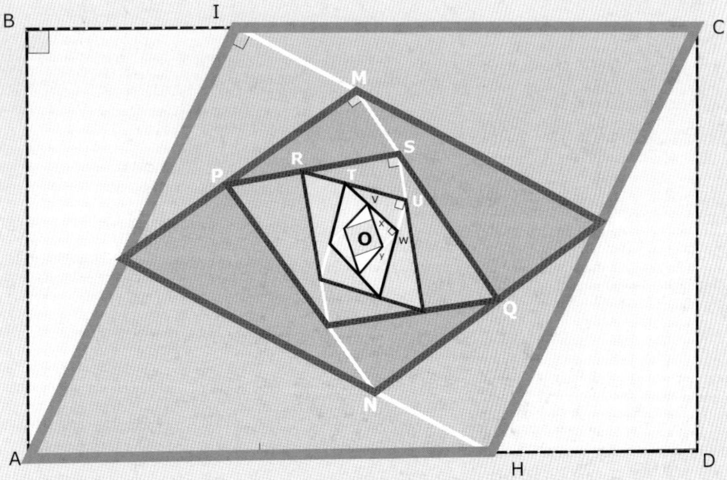

This drawing can also determine diamonds (6 in this figure) with the hypotenuses of the 4 L-shaped squares of each golden rectangle.

For example in the golden rectangle ABCD, diamond AICH then in JIKH, diamond JMKN etc...

In each diamond the ratio of the diagonals = Φ example: JK / MN = Φ.

FIG. 4-13 ~ Three ray star

Equilateral triangle and golden section

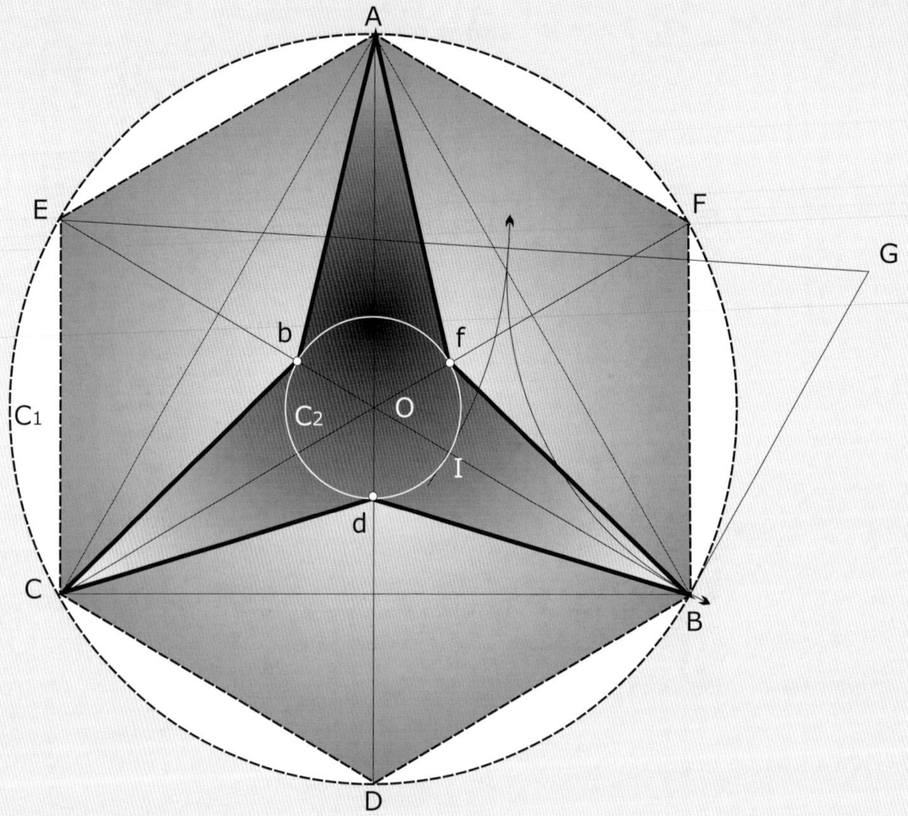

Consider the circle with O as center (C_1) and the regular hexagon AFBDCE inscribed in circle (C_1)
Draw ligne segments AC = CB = BA. Triangle ABC is equilateral.

Draw line segments AD, CF and BE.

From segment BE, draw the right triangle BGE that is right-angled at B
such as BG = BE / 2 (BEG is the 1/2 L-shaped square).

Point I divides segment BE according to mean and extreme ratio
$EI / IB = \Phi$ (1-11 page 23).

Draw the inner circle (C_2) with O as center and OI as radius.
The circle (C_2) intersects AD at "d", CF at "f" and BE at "b"
Join points Ab, bC, Cd, dB, Bf, fA.

You will thus build the three ray star AfBdCbA.

FIG. 4-14 ~ SEVEN RAY STAR BY MEANS OF THE GOLDEN SECTION

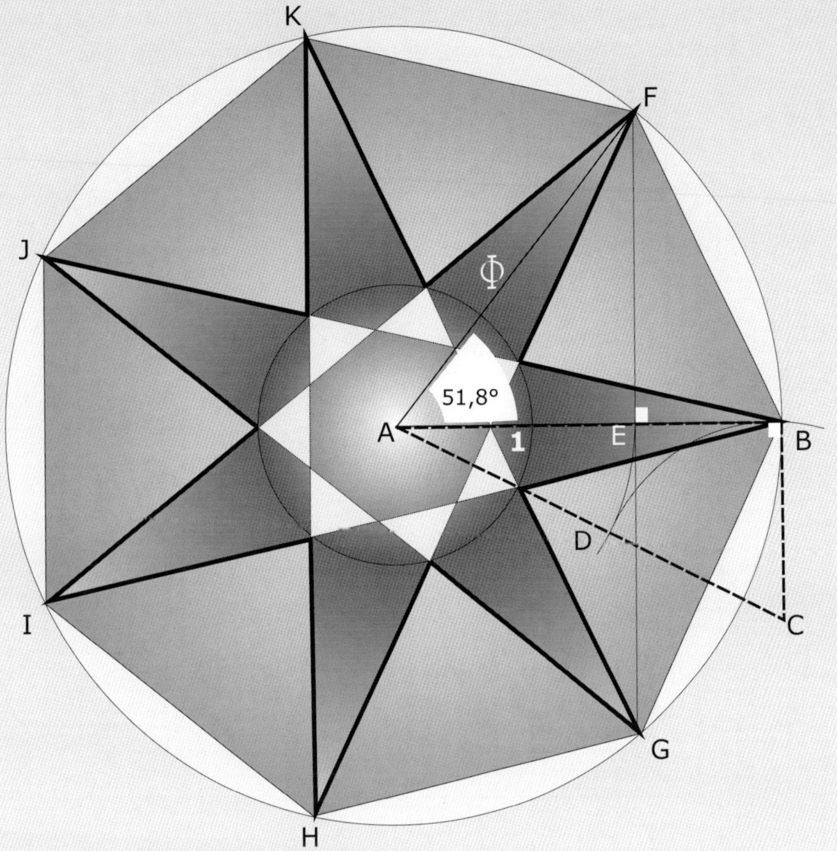

Consider the 1/2 L-shaped square ABC in which AB is divided according to mean and extreme ratio by point E (1-11 page 23 and 4-10 page 65), hence, AE / EB = AB / AE = Φ.

Draw the circle with A as center and AB as radius, it is the circle circumscribing the heptagon.

The line perpendicular to AB passing by E intersects circle A at F and G.

Segments FB = BG are the sides of the regular heptagon.

On the circumscribed circle draw chords GH = HI = IJ with BG
then, FK = KJ with BF which makes it possible to check the drawing at J.

The BGHIJKF heptagon has thus been built.

The star is built by joining together points K to G, K to H, F to I, F to H, B to J, B to I and G to J.

Note: 360 / 7 = 51.42° or angle BAF = 51.8° (Cheops angle).
There is an approximation of 0.4° so, point J must be checked and corrected if necessary.

FIG. 4-15 ~ "Φ" RAY STAR

The "cross patée", that is engraved on the right-hand pylon in the naos of the temple of Philae in Egypt and the cross that can also be found at St James of Compostella, would bear the same aspect as the figure below which is proper to the author of this book.

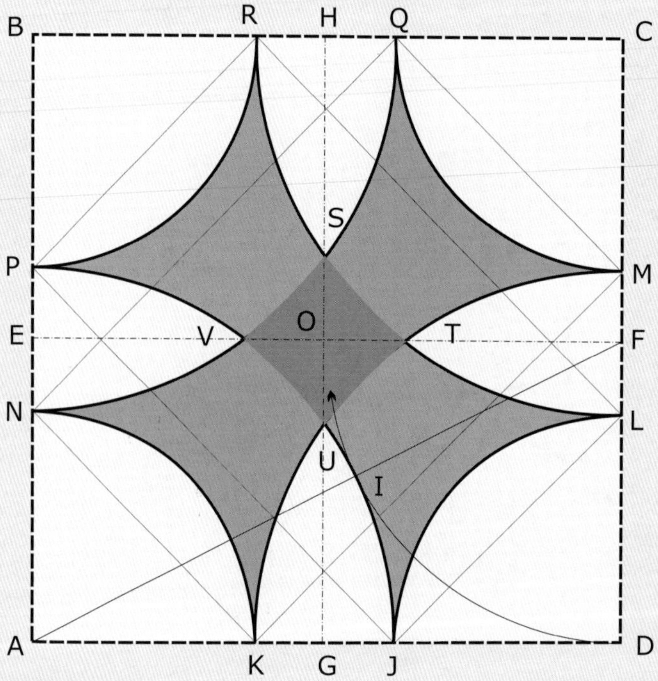

Consider square ABCD and points J and K that divide segment AD according to mean and extreme ratio AJ / JD = Φ and DK / KA = Φ.

Draw the arc with D as center and DJ as radius = r1 intersecting CD at L.

Draw the arc with D as center and DK as radius = r2 intersecting CD at M, GH at U and EF at T.

Draw the arc with A as center and AK as radius = r1 intersecting AB at N.

Draw the arc with A as center and AJ as radius = r2 intersecting AB at P, EF at V.

Do the same for the B and C vertexes of square ABCD.

The KNPRQMLJ star has thus been built.

Notes: — the broken arcs TML, KUJ, NVP and RSQ bear a Φ ratio Indeed TL / ML = Φ.

— The equal rectangles PRLJ and QMKN are golden rectangles.

FIG. 4-16 ~ "Φ" 4 RAY STAR OR CROSS PATEE

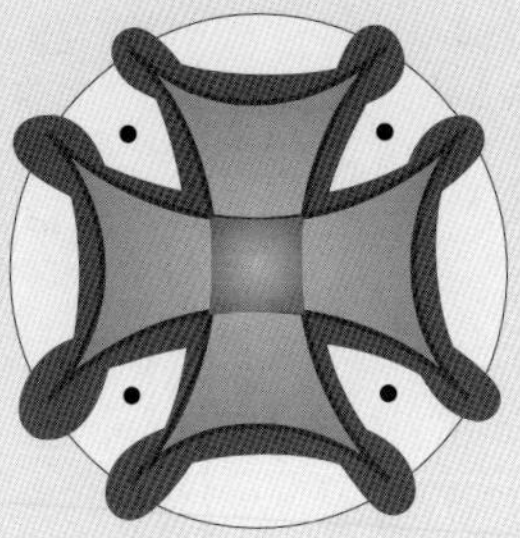

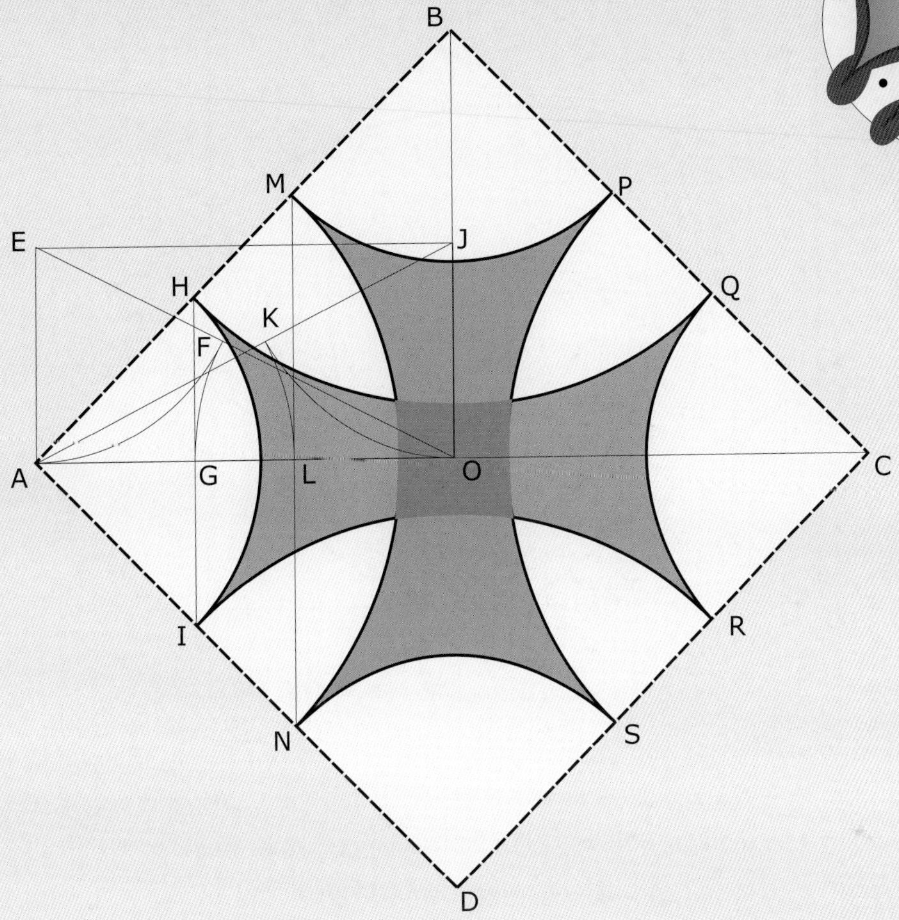

Consider square ABCD and O the center of the circumscribed circle.

G and L divide OA according to mean and extreme ratio
such as OG / GA = LA / OL = Φ (figures obtained with the 1/2 L-shaped squares OAE and AOJ).

The perpendicular to OA passing by G intersects the sides of the square at H and I.

The perpendicular to OA passing by L intersects the sides of the square at M and N.

The arc with A as center and AH = r_1 as radius determines arc HI
and the arc with AM = r_2 as radius determines arc MN.

Similarly, draw the arcs with B as center, then C and lastly D with radii r_1 and r_2.

You will thus determine the "cross patée" or four ray star.

FIG. 4-17 ~ Romanesque and Gothic mandorlas ("vesica pisces")

Figure drawn by means of a square

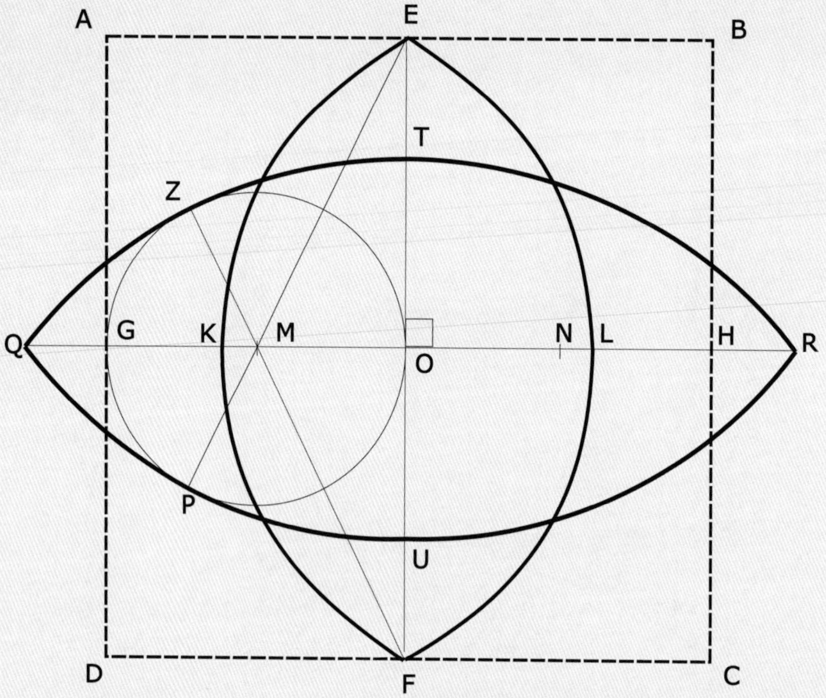

Consider square ABCD, side = 2. Its medians EF and GH intersect at O.

Romanesque mandorla: Place points M and N, respectively centers of GO and OH.

Draw the arc with M as center and ME as radius intersecting GH at L, that is to say arc ELF.

Draw the arc with N as center and NE as radius intersecting GH at K, that is to say arc FKE.

Thus we obtain the Romanesque mandorla ELFKE.

This mandorla is inscribed in a golden rectangle, EF / KL = 1.618 = Φ.

Gothic mandorla (with the golden section as radius):

Draw the circle with M as center and MO as radius intersecting EM at P and FM at Z.

Draw the arc with E as center and EP as radius intersecting straight line GH at Q and R, that is to say arc RPQ.

Draw the arc with F as center and FZ as radius that intersects straight line GH at Q and R, that is to say arc QZR.

You will thus obtain the Gothic mandorla RPQZR whose radii PE and FZ = Φ.

This mandorla is inscribed in a rectangle; the ratio of the sides is QR / TU = $\Phi \times \sqrt{\Phi} = 2.06$

Note: The Φ values for the Romanesque mandorla and ($\Phi \times \sqrt{\Phi}$) for the Gothic mandorla, characterise the Romanesque and Gothic tympanums.

fig. 4-18 ~ Gothic mandorla

figure drawn by means of a regular decagon

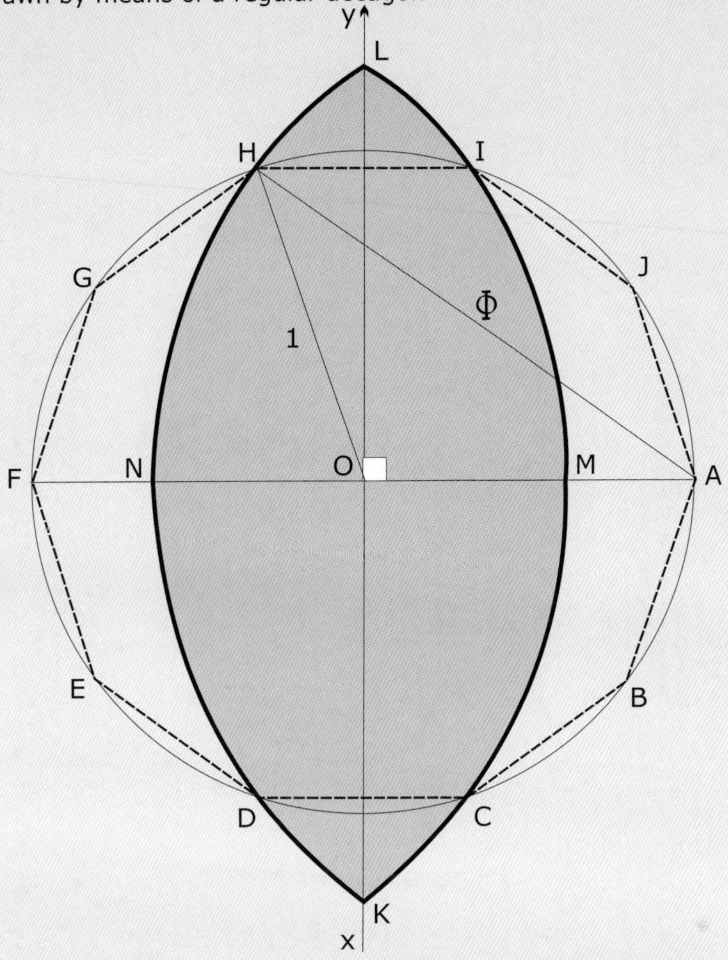

Consider the regular decagon ABCDEFGHIJ (3-06 page 45).

Draw the circle, circumscribing the regular decagon, with O as center and draw the straight line xy perpendicular to diameter AF.

Draw the arc with F as center and FI as radius that intersects xy at L and K, and AF at M determining arc LIMCK.

Draw the arc with A as center and AH as radius that intersects xy at L and K and AF at N determining arc KDNHL.

Arcs LIMCK and KDNHL constitute the two arcs of the Gothic mandorla.

Notes: - AH, the radius of arc KDNHL and HO, the radius of the circle circumscribing the regular decagon, bear a Φ ratio.

- AH / HO = Φ, AOH is the divine triangle (4-04 page 59).
- O divides line segment AN according to mean and extreme ratio AO / ON = Φ.
- LK / MN has a value close to 2.

FIG. 4-19 ~ DRAWING AN EGG

starting from a regular pentagon

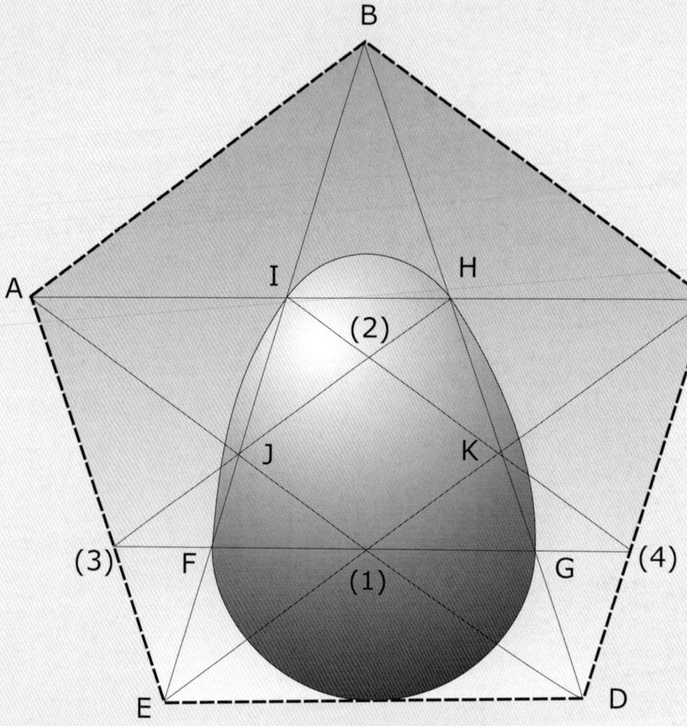

Consider the regular pentagon ABCDE (3-01 page 40).

Diagonal AC intersects BE at I and BD at H.

Diagonals AD and CE intersect at point (1).

Diagonals BE and AD intersect at J.

Diagonals BD and CE intersect at K.

HJ intersects AE at (3) and IK intersects CD at (4).

The straight line (3-4) intersects BE at F and BD at G and furthermore it passes by (1).
Segments (3)H and (4)1 intersect at point (2).

Draw the semi-circle with (1) as center and FG as diameter.
Draw the arc with (2) as center and (2)I as radius, that is to say arc IH.
Draw the arc with (3) as center and (3)H as radius, that is to say arc HG.
Draw the arc with (4) as center and (4)F as radius, that is to say arc FI.

The FIHGF egg has been built.

Looking for the 6th solid: a kit or a kite?

the platonic solids

5

FIG. 5-01 ~ REGULAR CONVEX POLYHEDRONS INSCRIBED IN A SPHERE (PLATONIC SOLIDS)

In the 5th century B.C, PLATO proved the existence of solid figures having regular polygonal and equal faces as well as equal angles at the vertexes.
Such solids, called regular polyhedrons are said to be convex if they can rest wholly upon one side of the plane of any of their faces. Plato counted five.
Each one is inscribed in a sphere and has an inscribed sphere that is tangential to all their faces.

Ancient mathematicians such as EUCLID, ARCHIMEDES, APPOLONIUS, also studied them; so did Albert DURER in the Middle Ages, Leonardo DA VINCI in the Renaissance and later, in the 16th, 17th and 18th centuries, KEPLER, EULER, POINSOT, CAUCHY, CATALAN, Joseph BERTRAND ...

the five platonic solids

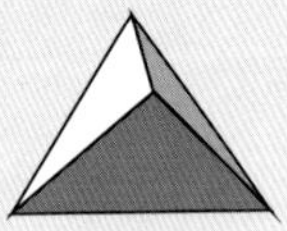

TETRAHEDRON
- 4 faces (equilateral triangles)
- 4 vertexes
- 6 edges

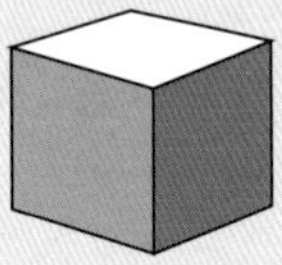

HEXAHEDRON or CUBE
- 6 square faces
- 8 vertexes
- 12 edges

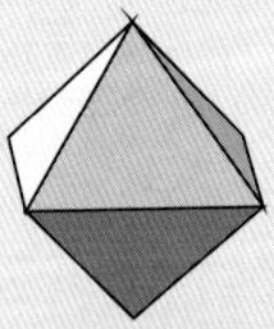

OCTAHEDRON
- 8 faces (equilateral triangles)
- 6 vertexes
- 12 edges

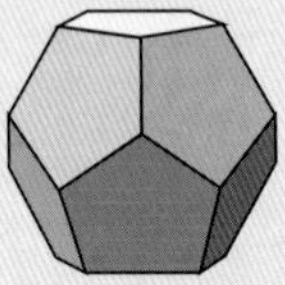

DODECAHEDRON
- 12 faces (pentagons)
- 20 vertexes
- 30 edges

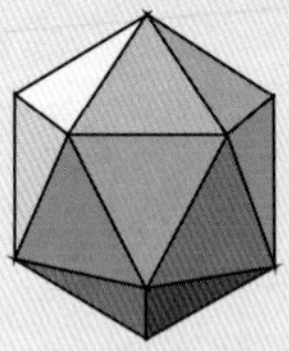

ICOSAHEDRON
- 20 faces (equilateral triangles)
- 12 vertexes
- 30 edges

Euler's formula can be verified for each solid: F (faces), V (vertexes), E (edges)

$$F + V = E + 2$$

FIG. 5-02 ~ TETRAHEDRON AND INVERTED TETRAHEDONS INSCRIBED IN A CUBE

Tetrahedron "A"

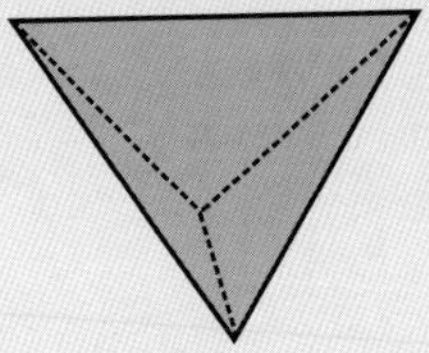

Tetrahedron "B"

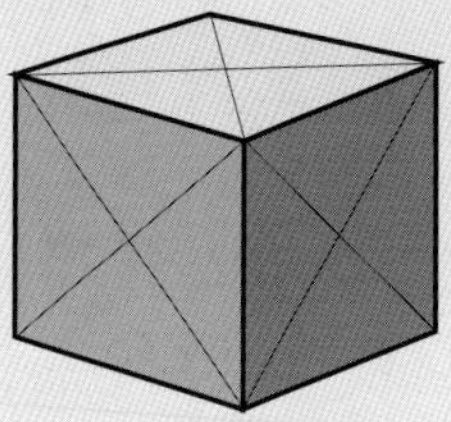

Cube, side = a

Tetrahedron "A" inscribed in the cube:

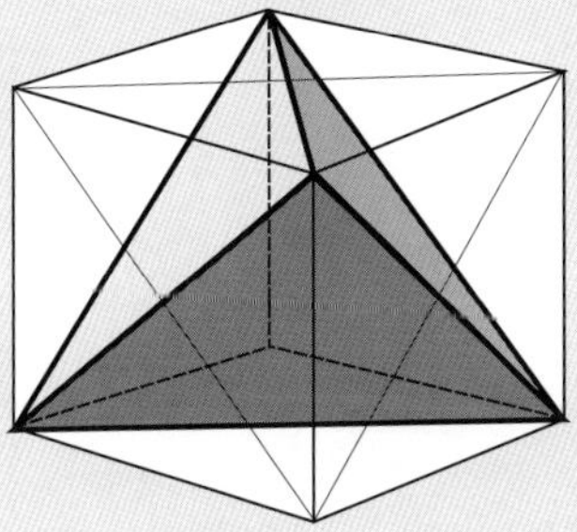

Its four vertexes are common to the four vertexes of the cube and its six edges are common to the 12 diagonals of the faces of the cube. The edge of the tetrahedron = a x$\sqrt{2}$

Tetrahedron "A" and inverted tetrahedron "B" inscribed in the cube:

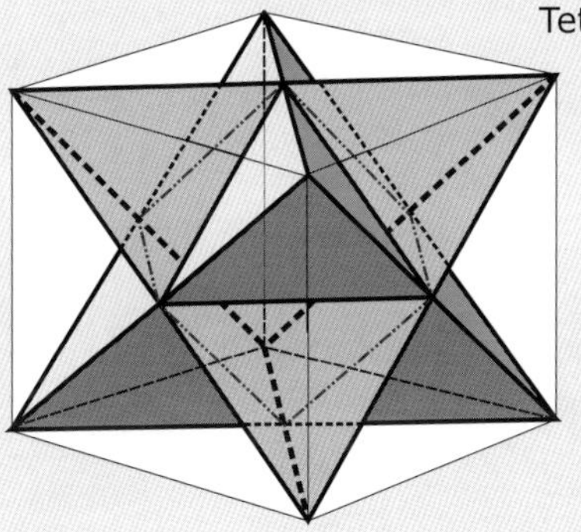

— "B" occupies the 4 vertexes and the 6 unoccupied diagonals of the cube.
— "A" and "B" constitute a new solid, an 8 point star inscribed in the cube, called "**stella octangula**".

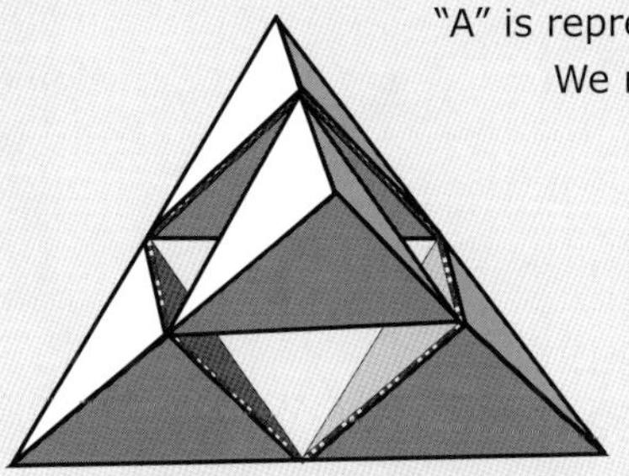

"A" is represented here without the part it has in common with "B".
We notice that it is constituted of 4 equal tetrahedons, whose edges = (a x $\sqrt{2}$) / 2.

The part which is common to the two inverted tetrahedrons "A" and "B" has of course vertexes situated at the intersections of the diagonals of the faces of the cube.

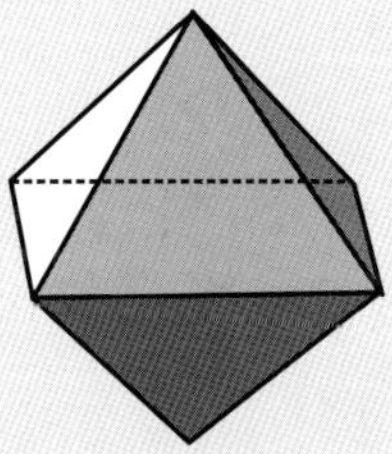

It is an octahedron inscribed in the cube, see 5-04 page 79.

Fig. 5-03 ~ Hexahedron or Cube Inscribed in a Sphere

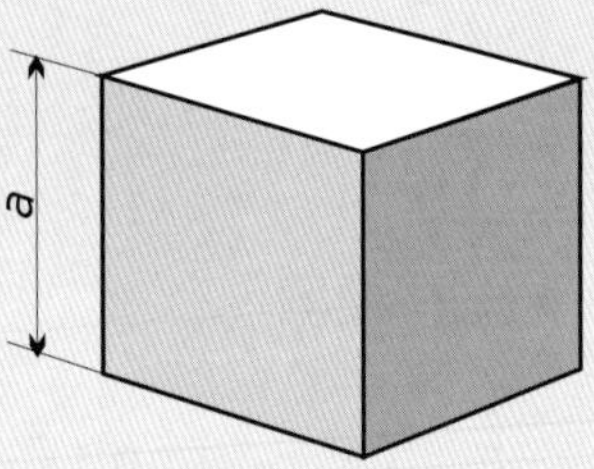

The cube seen in perspective.

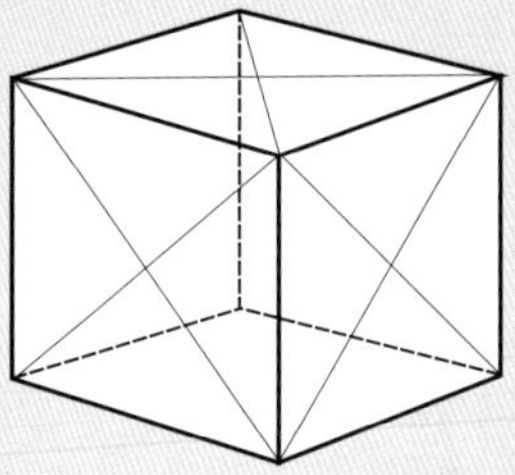

The cube with the diagonals of its three visible faces and the dotted line of its unseen edges.

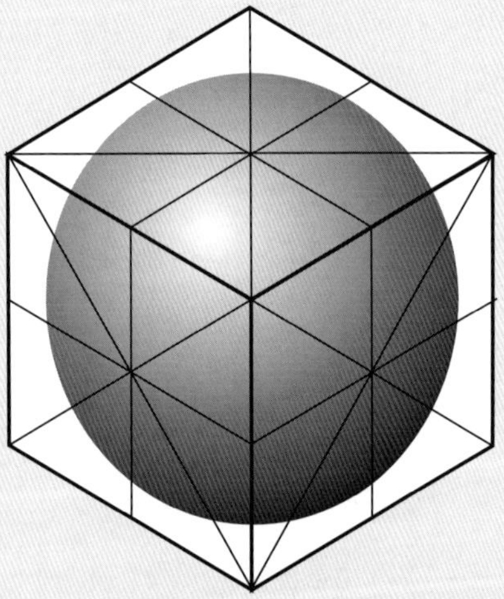

The sphere inscribed in the cube has a diameter that is equal to the edge of the cube, it has six points of contact with the centers of the six faces of the cube.

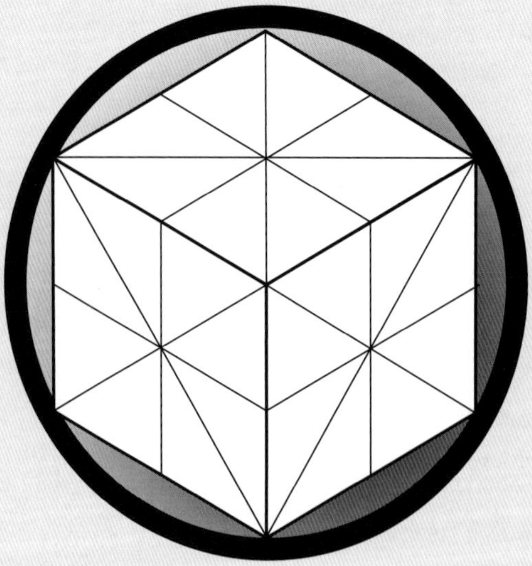

The cube inscribed in a sphere has six points of contact with the sphere by its six vertexes. The diameter of the sphere, said to be "circumscribed" to the cube, is equal to $a\sqrt{3}$.

The inscribed sphere, the circumscribed sphere and the cube are concentric.

FIG. 5-04 ~ OCTAHEDRON INSCRIBED IN A CUBE AND IN A SPHERE

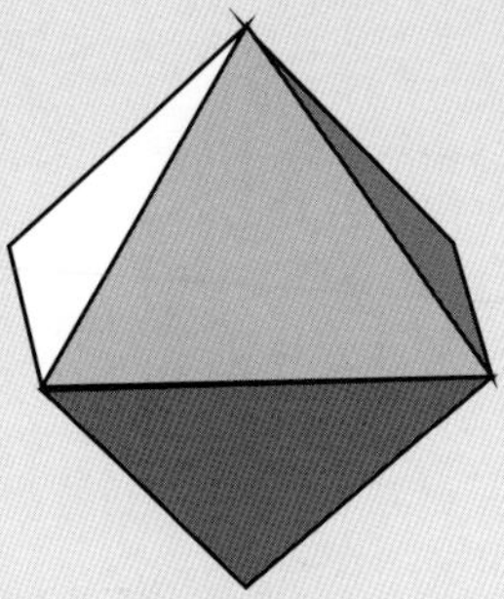

a

The octahedron is the polyhedron we met at 5-02, page 77, with its eight triangular faces, its 6 vertexes and its 12 edges.

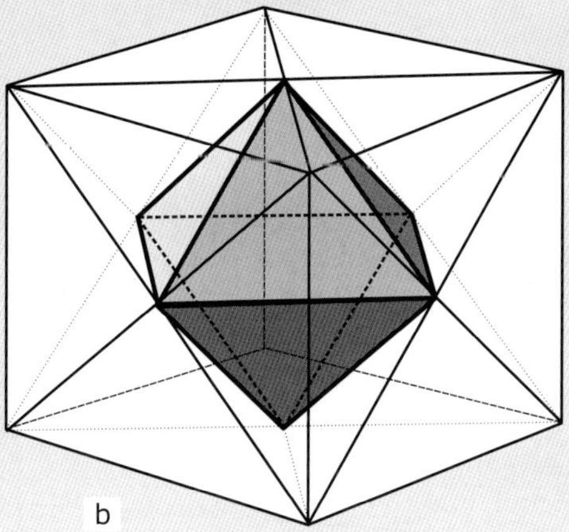

b

The octahedron inscribed in a cube has 6 vertexes centered on the 6 faces of the cube: that is what brings about the "dual relationships" between the octahedron and the cube.

By joining the centers of the 8 faces of the octahedron, we obtain an inscribed cube.

Note that any platonic solid has another "**dual**" platonic solid whose vertexes are centered on its faces.

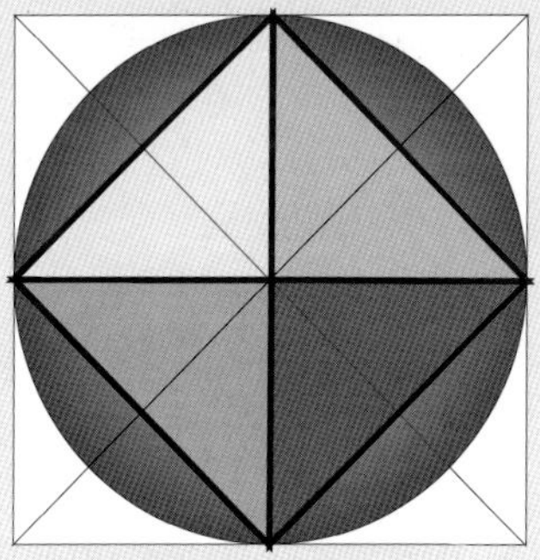

c

The octahedron seen from any of the 6 faces of the cube.

The octahedron inscribed in the cube will also be inscribed in the sphere with a diameter = a that is itself inscribed in the cube as seen at 5-03, page 78.

Octahedron, cube and sphere are concentric.

Reciprocity of the cube and of the octahedron (duality).
The 6 faces of the cube correspond to the 6 vertexes of the octahedron.
The 8 vertexes of the cube correspond to the 8 faces of the octahedron.
The 12 edges of the cube correspond to the 12 orthogonal edges of the octahedron.

Fig. 5-05 ~ Dodecahedron inscribed in a cube and a sphere

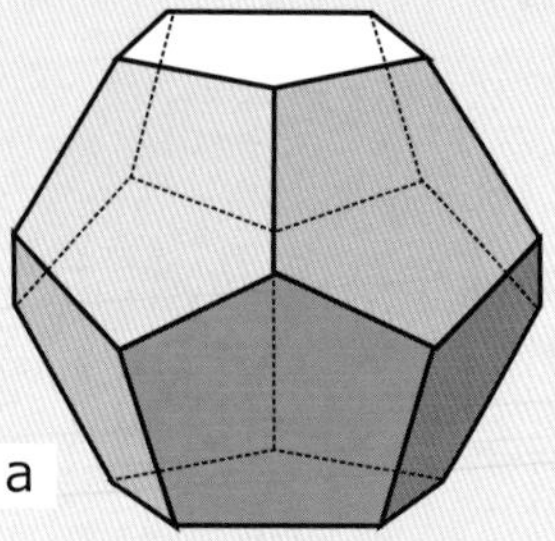

a

A dodecahedron has:
12 parallel faces two by two equidistant from the center
30 parallel edges two by two
20 vertexes equidistant from the center.

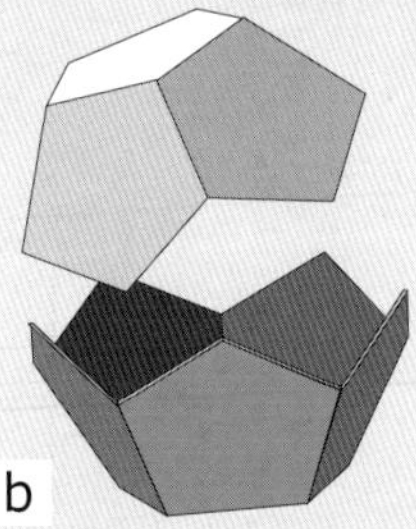

b

The dodecahedron can be separated into two identical parts.

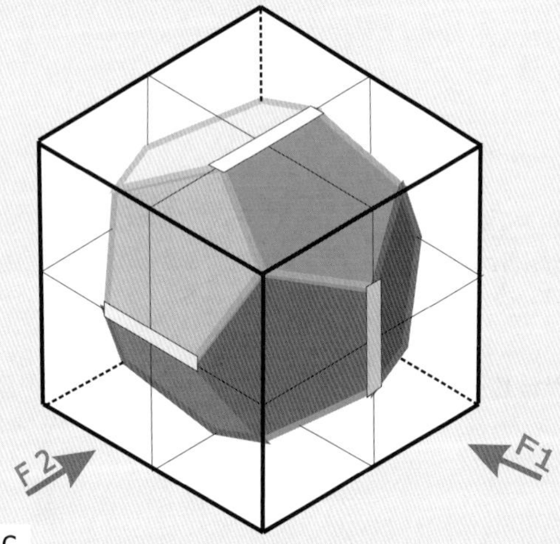

c

The dodecahedron is inscribed in a cube with side = a. It is in contact with this cube by 6 edges (we have marked the three that are visible by a pale gray rectangle).

There is no duality between these two solids as the 20 vertexes of the dodecahedron cannot correspond to the centers of 20 faces, a cube having only 6 faces.

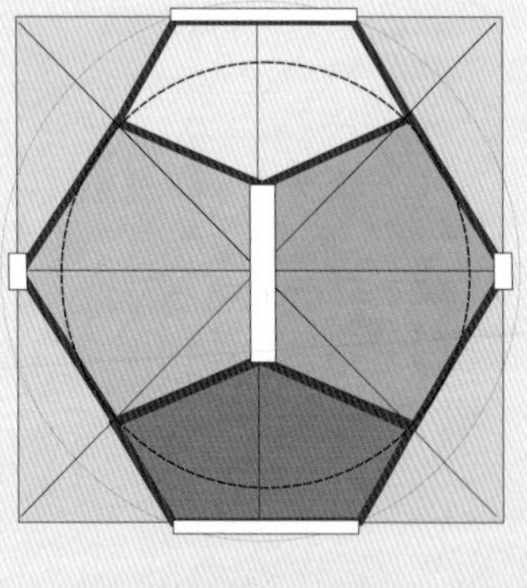

d

The dodecahedron seen according to arrow F1 in its cube with side = a
The sphere circumscribed to the dodecahedron is not inscribed in the cube.

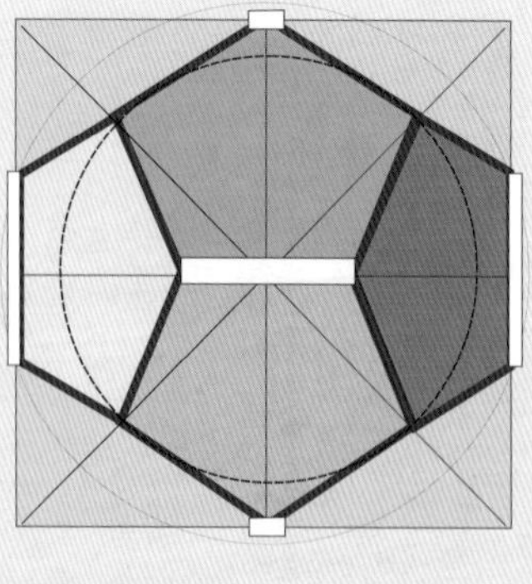

e

The dodecahedron seen according to arrow F2. The sphere inscribed in the dodecahedron is in contact with the centers of its 12 faces.

Dodecahedron, cube and sphere are concentric.

FIG. 5-06 ~ ICOSAHEDRON INSCRIBED IN A CUBE AND A SPHERE

For each of these three rectangles: length / width = Φ.

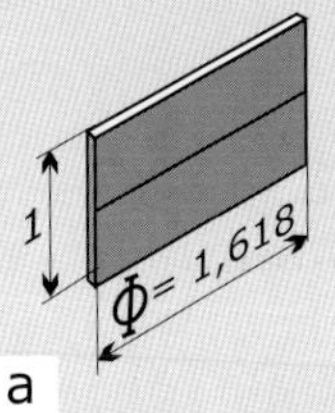

a

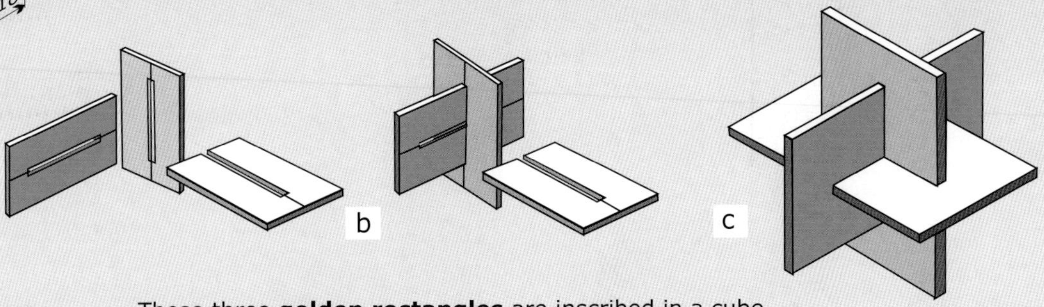

b

c

These three **golden rectangles** are inscribed in a cube.

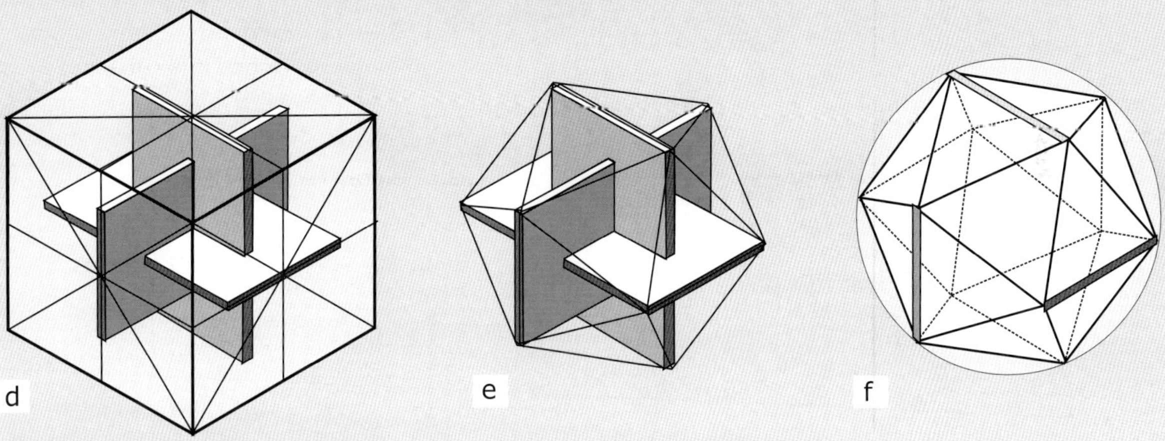

d

e

f

A thread joining the (3 x 4) vertexes of the golden rectangles e, brings into existence an **icosahedron** (12 vertexes, 20 faces and 30 edges =1) that bears a clear relationship to **Φ.**

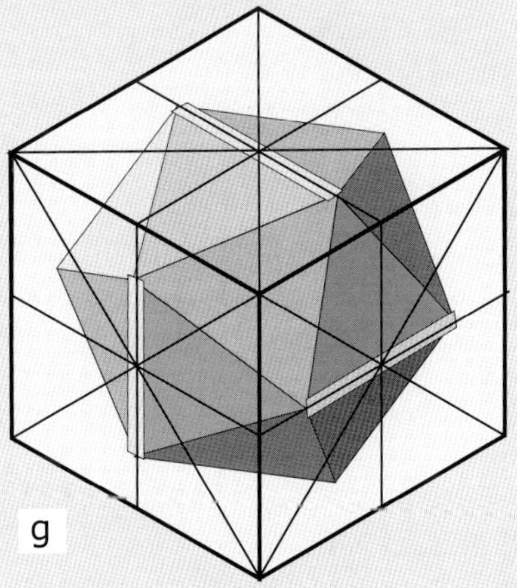

g

The **icosahedron** is inscribed in cube g
with side a = Φ
and in sphere f
whose diameter = the length of the golden rectangle.

These three solids are concentric.

Fig. 5-07~ Relationships between dodecahedron, icosahedron and the golden section

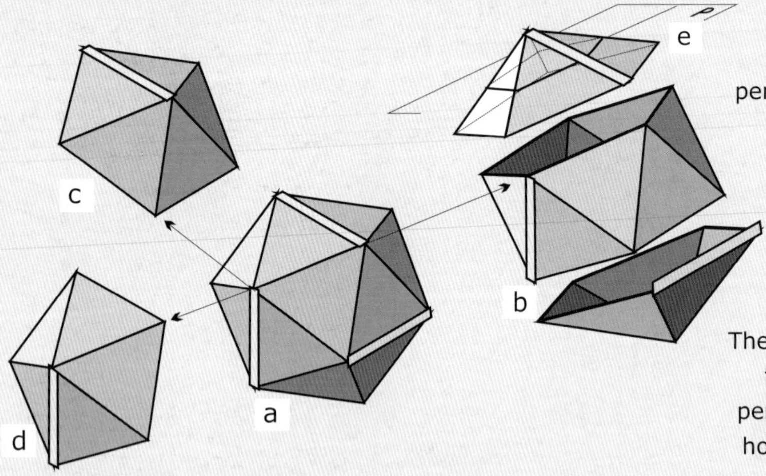

Any plane P, parallel to the pentagonal base of the pyramid, cuts this pyramid forming a pentagon.

The **icosahedron** is composed of two pyramids with inverted pentagonal bases and a hoop of 10 equilateral triangles alternating top to base.

c and d are pyramids with pentagonal bases that can be separated from the icosahedron by any of its 12 vertexes.

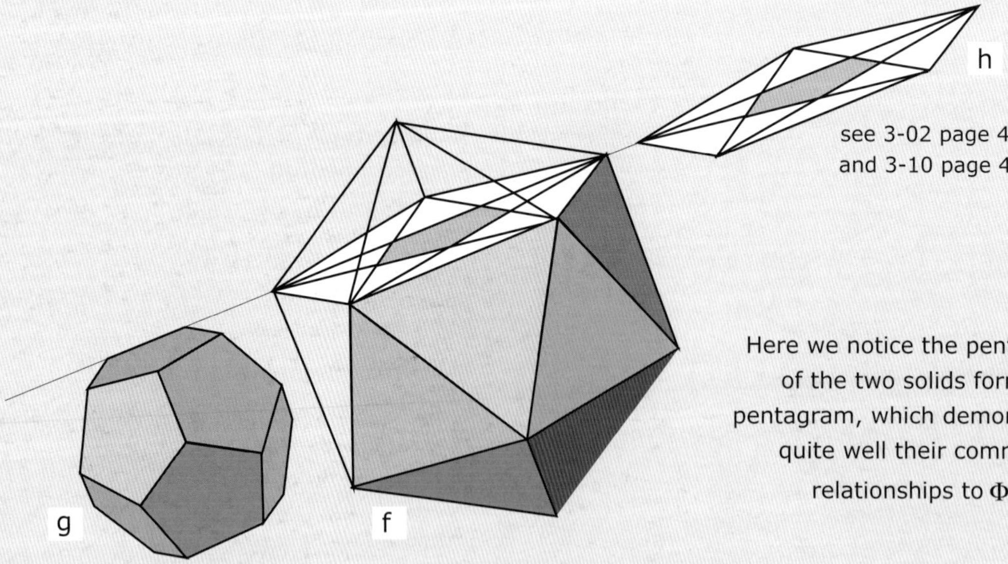

see 3-02 page 41
and 3-10 page 49

Here we notice the pentagons of the two solids form a pentagram, which demonstrates quite well their common relationships to **Φ.**

FIG. 5-08 ~ Relationships between dodecahedron, icosahedron and the golden section

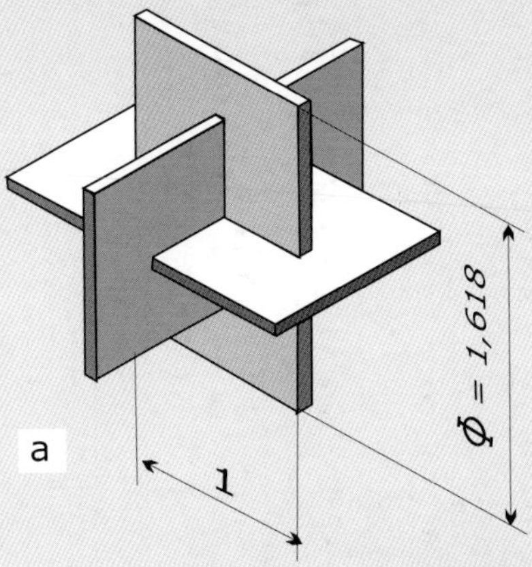

a

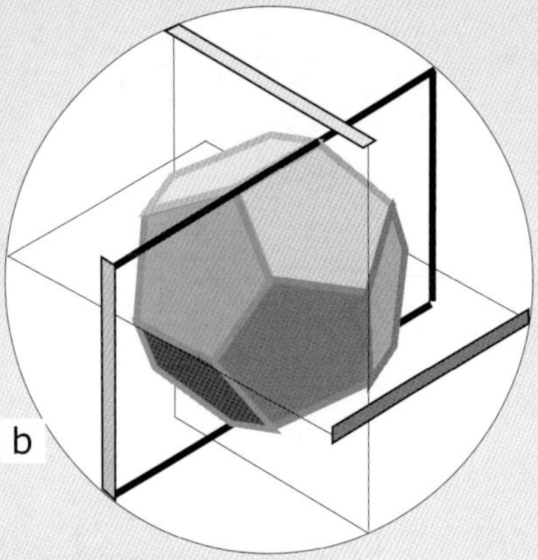

b

Let's place the dodecahedron (5-05 page 80) in the center of the sphere inscribing the three golden rectangles that make up the icosahedron (5-06 page 81).

The figures f , g , h of 5-07 page 82 and the ones on this page show quite evidently the relationships between the cube,the icosahedron, the dodecahedron, and the golden section Φ.

The cross section of b made by the plan of the vertical rectangle of a reveals the dodecahedron inscribed in the cube with side a = 1 (5-05 page 80).

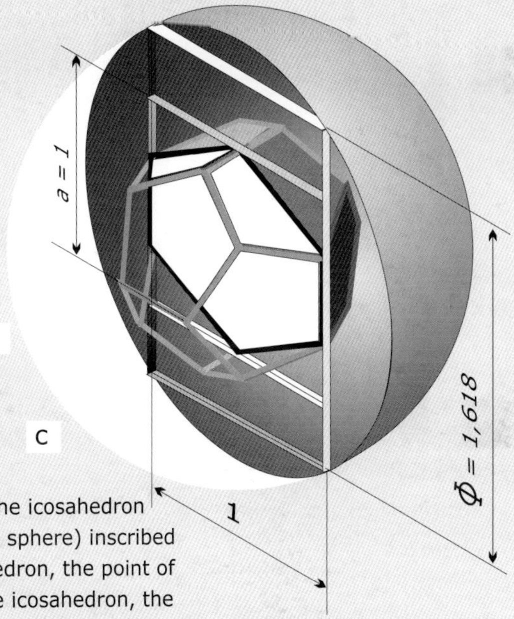

c

Let's show that the icosahedron can also be (with its sphere) inscribed in another dodecahedron, the point of contact between the icosahedron, the dodecahedron-sphere being at the center of the faces of this dodecahedron, hence the duality of these two solids.

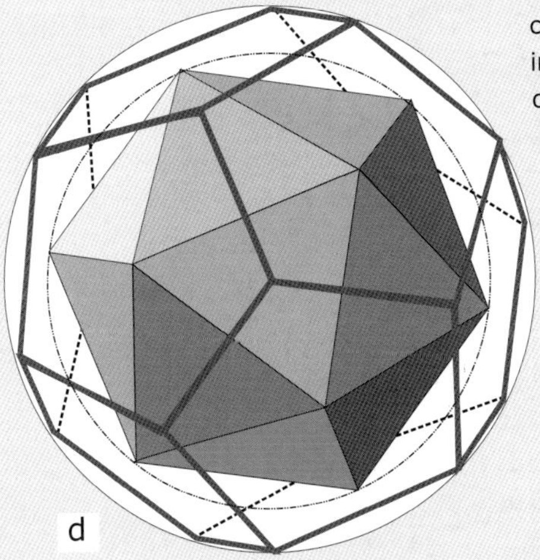

d

Reciprocal points of that duality

dodecahedron	icosahedron
12 faces ↔	12 vertexes
20 vertexes ↔	20 faces
30 edges ↔	30 perpendicular edges

fig. 5-09 ~ platonic solids and the golden section

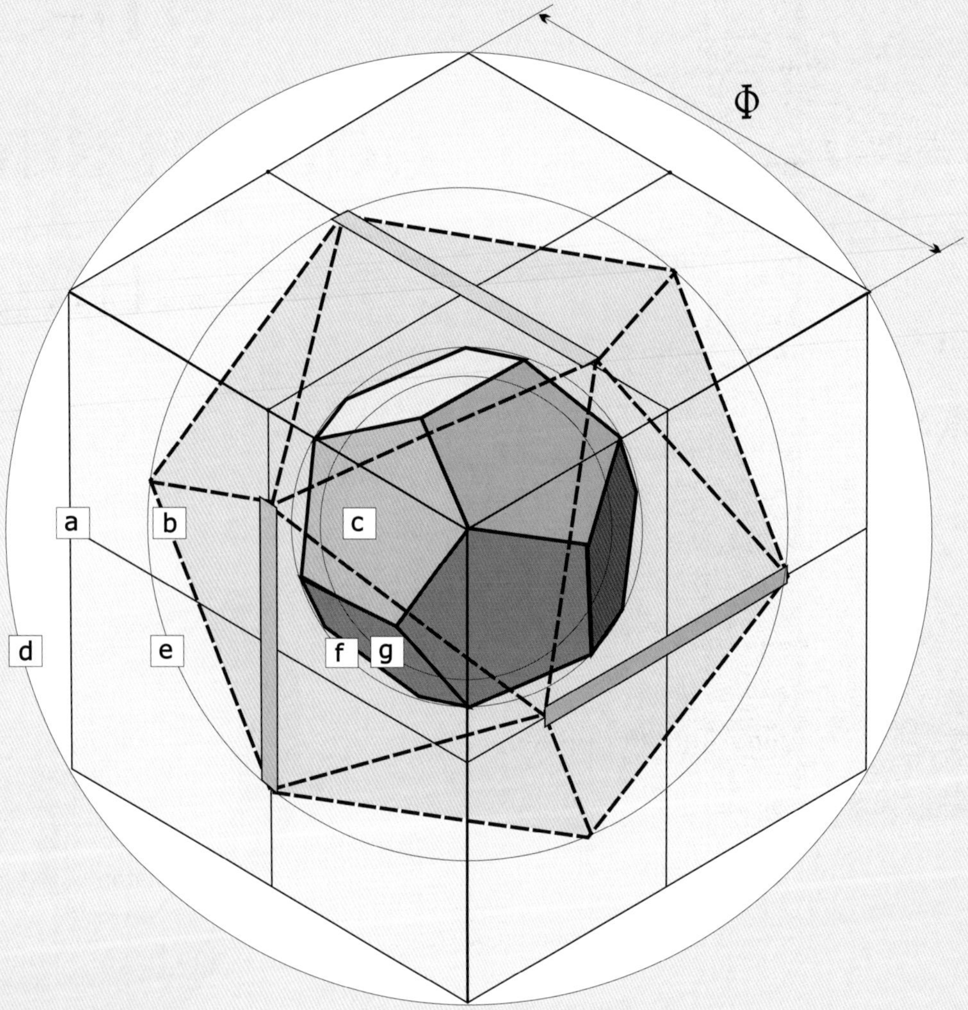

Consider the
three following solids: cube a , icosahedron b and dodecahedron c

and the spheres: d sphere circumscibing the cube

e sphere circumscribing the icosahedron

f sphere circumscribing the dodecahedron

g sphere inscribed in the dodecahedron

Let's imagine the cube, side a' = 1 (the one which inscribes the dodecahedron 5-05c p; 80 and 5-08b p. 83).
We can thus see three golden rectangles (5-06c page 81) and the relationship with Φ
the side of the cube a = Φ
That same cube, inscribing the tetrahedron and the octahedron,
also shows us the relationships between those two solids.

Façade of the "Chateau des Papes" in Avignon

the golden section in human achievements

6

Fig. 6-01 ~ the Cheops pyramid

Perspective by location of the golden triangles.

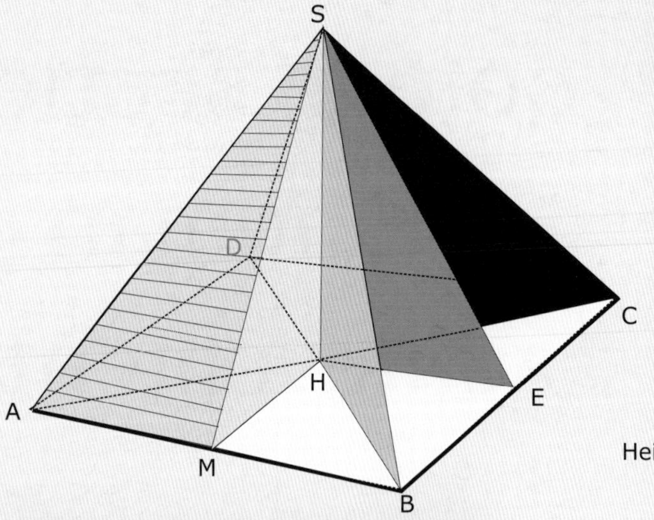

Base square ABCD, side = 2
Edges SA = SB = SC = SD = $\sqrt{(\Phi + 2)}$
Apothems SM = SE = SF = Φ
Height SH = $\sqrt{\Phi}$

Right triangle AMS - 6-02
Right triangle SHE - 6-03
Right triangle SHB - 6-04
Values of SA and SM - 6-05

Length of the side of the base square:
435 cubits i.e. 229 meters.

Height of the pyramid 280 cubits i.e. 147 meters.

The pyramid in the court of the Louvre Museum in Paris, designed by architect I.M. PEI, has much smaller dimensions than that of Cheops but it has the same proportions and so the same angles and the same relationship to the golden section.

The geometric figures we propose hereafter are valid for both pyramids separated by "only" nearly 4500 years.

Fig. 6-02 ~ Cheops pyramid, drawing of triangle AMS

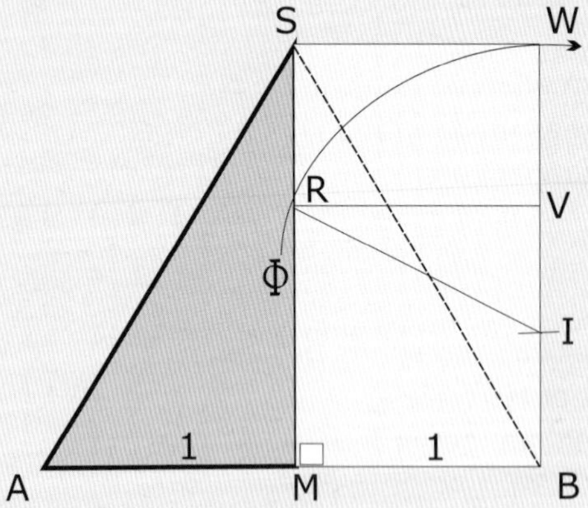

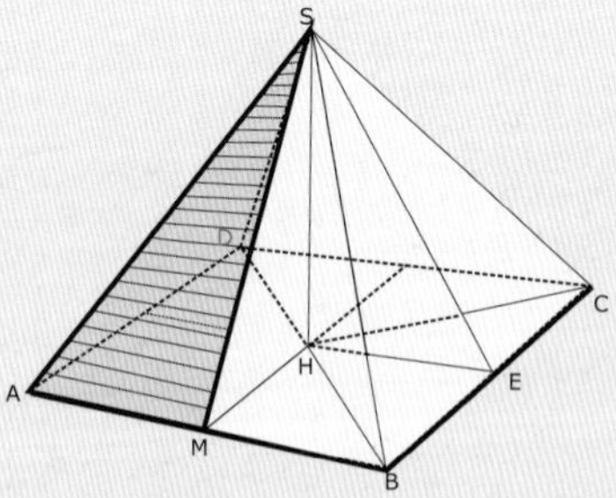

Triangle ASB is viewed in a vertical plane.

Consider the drawing of Φ with the fundamental square RVBM.
The right triangle ASM, right-angled at M, is such that:

SM = Φ, AM = 1 and AS = $\sqrt{(\Phi + 2)}$

The isosceles triangle ASB has an AB base = 2
and sides, SB = AS.

fig. 6-03 ~ the cheops pyramid

Drawing the right triangle SHE

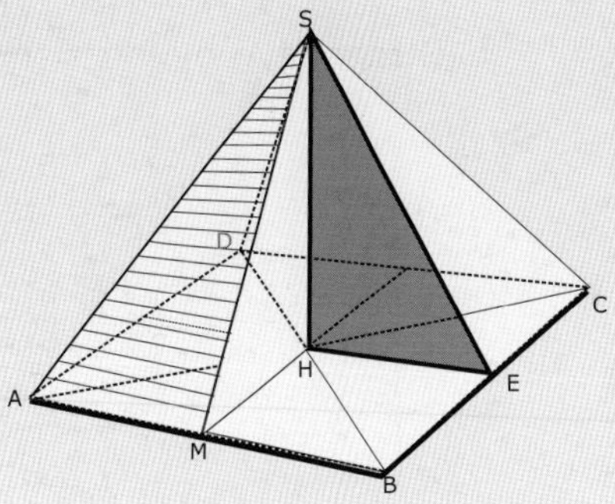

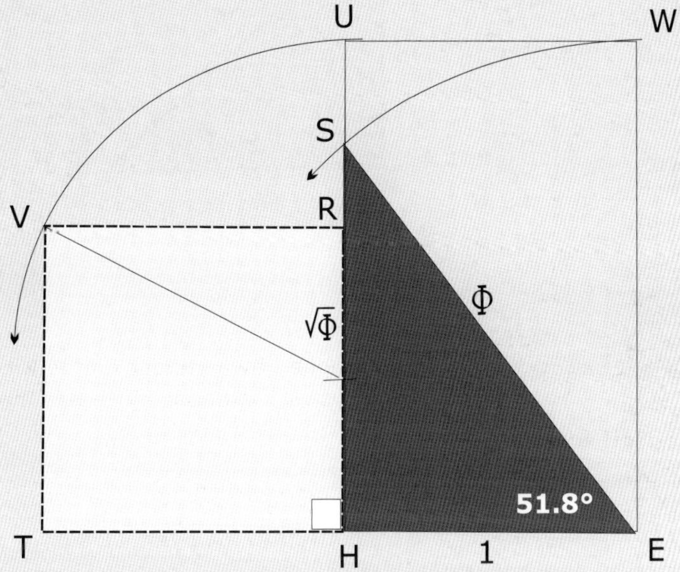

Consider the fundamental square HTVR, side = 1.

Draw HU = Φ.

Draw the arc with H as center and HT = 1 as radius intersecting TH at E.

On the perpendicular to UH, from point U, draw UW = 1
You have EW = Φ.

Draw the arc with E as center and EW = Φ as radius intersecting UH at S.

You have obtained the right triangle SHE that is right-angled at H.
Its characteristics are:
SE = Φ, HE = 1 and SH = $\sqrt{\Phi}$

Note: the angle of the apothem (ES) to the ground (angle SEH) is about 51.8°.

FIG. 6-04 ~ the cheops pyramid

Drawing the right triangle SHB

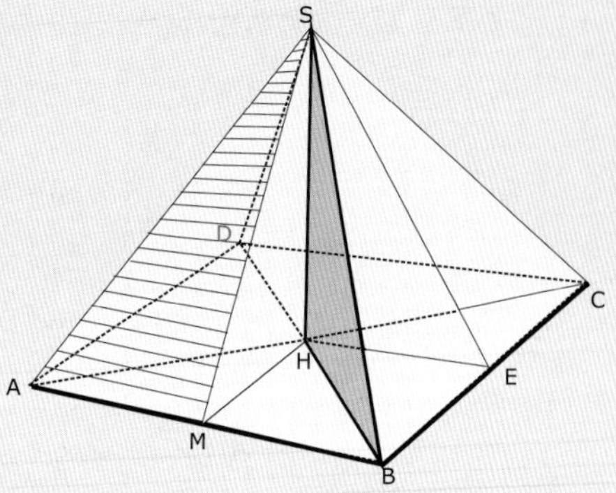

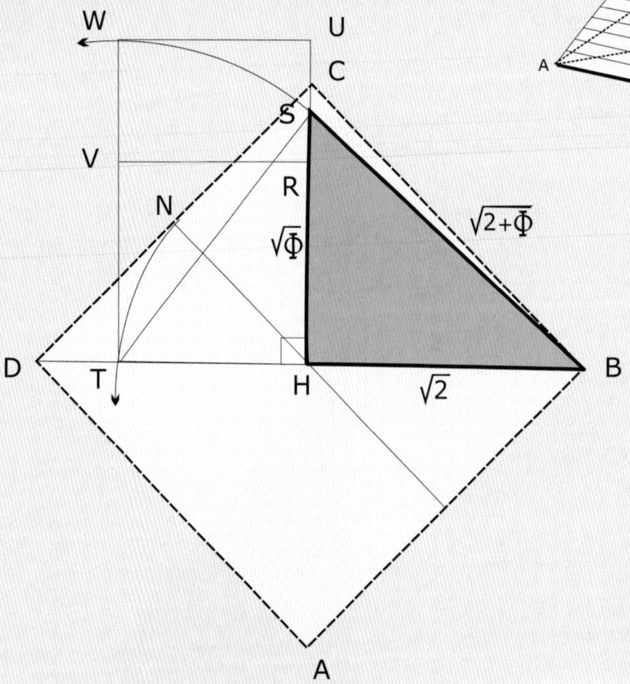

Consider the square base ADCB of the pyramid, side = 2,
H is the point of convergence of the diagonals and N is the middle of DC
The right triangle SHB is viewed in a horizontal plane.

Draw the arc with H as center and HN as radius
intersecting segment DB at T, NH = TH = 1.

Draw Φ with the fundamental square HTVR
HU = TW = Φ.

Draw the arc with T as center and WT = Φ as radius intersecting HC at S.

You have thus built the right triangle HSB, right-angled at H.
Its hypotenuse is
$SB = \sqrt{2 + \Phi}$
and its sides $SH = \sqrt{\Phi}$ and $HB = \sqrt{2}$.

Note: the angle of the edge (BS) to the ground (angle SBH) is about 42°.

fig. 6-05 ~ the Cheops pyramid - descriptive geometry - development

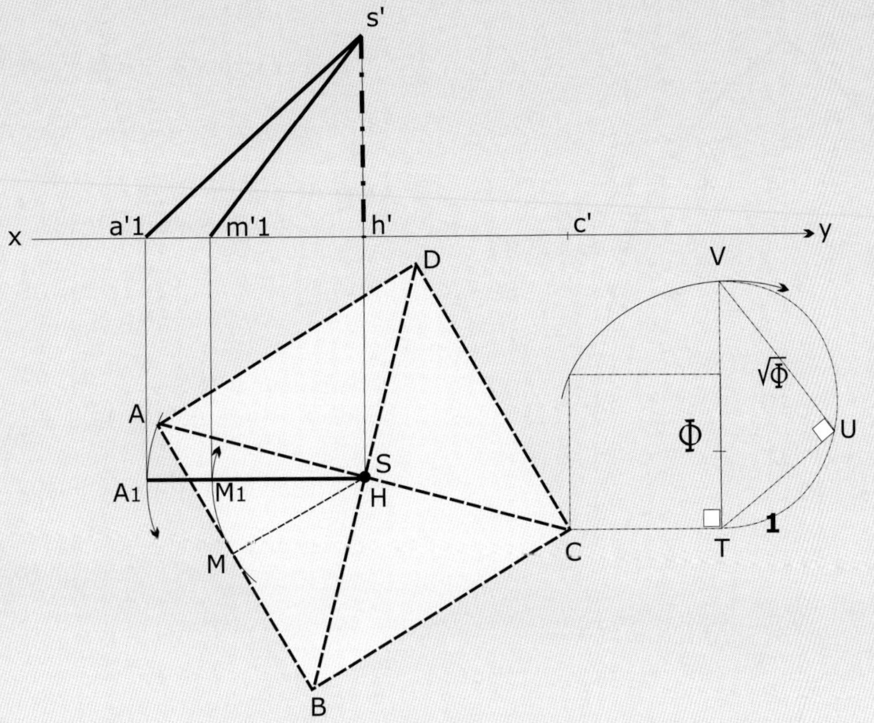

Consider the Cheops pyramid viewed from above with its base ABCD, side = 2, its vertex S and the starting point of its height H (they are undistinguished as they are situated on the same vertical)
Draw Φ with the fundamental square, side CT = 1,
$UV = \sqrt{\Phi}$, TU = 1 and TV = Φ
UV is the height of the pyramid, $HS = UV = \sqrt{\Phi}$
that we raise in "true dimensions" in h's' above line xy, called "earth line".

To determine the true dimensions of edge SA and of apothem SM, bring those lines into a plane parallel to xy, by " rotation" around height SH according to the following process:

On the horizontal projection (ABCD, H, S, M)
- draw a circle with H as center and HA as radius intersecting the horizontal line, passing by H, at A1 (transferred to a'1 onto the "earth line" xy)
s'a'1 = true dimension of edge $SA = \sqrt{\Phi + 2}$.

- draw an arc with H as center and HM as radius intersecting the horizontal line, passing by H, at M1 (transferred onto m'1 on xy)
s'm'1 = SM = true dimension of the apothem, SM = Φ.

Fig. 6-06 ~ Drawing an arch: the ideal pointed arch

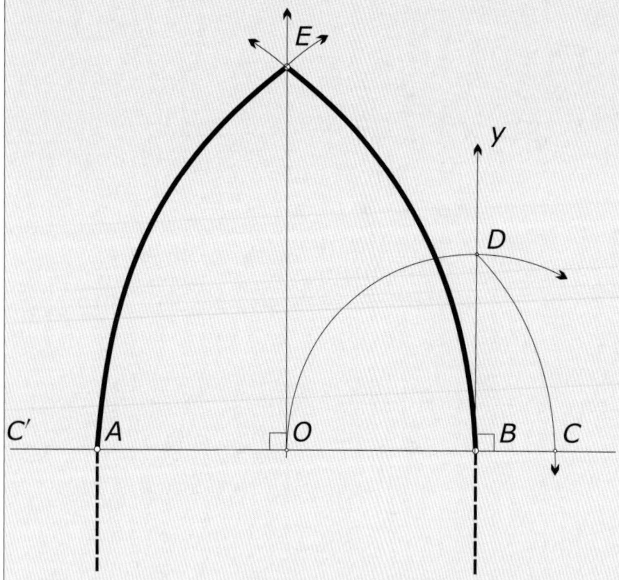

Consider span AB. O is the middle of AB.

From B, drop the perpendicular By to AB.

Draw an arc with B as center, BO as radius, intersecting By at D.

Draw an arc with O as center, OD as radius, intersecting AB at C.

Draw an arc with C as center, CA as radius, intersecting AB at E.

Arc EB is determined by symmetry to axis OE.

The pointed arch (ideal ogive) has thus been built.

Note: calculation shows that EO = AB, approximately.

Fig. 6-07~ Blunt arch

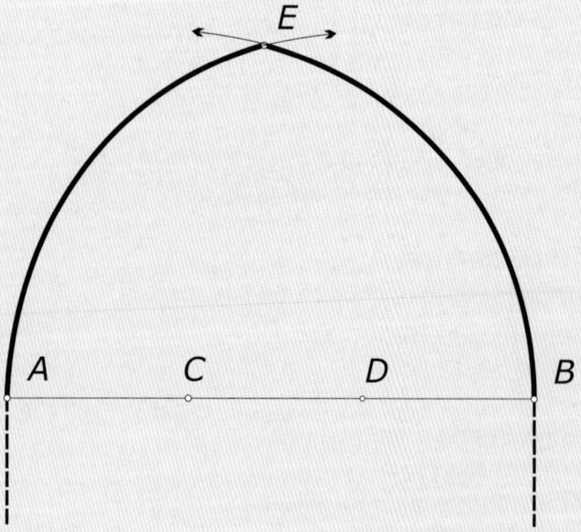

Consider span AB.

Divide line segment AB into three equal parts (1-08 page 21) AC = CD = DB = AB/3.

Draw the arc with C as center and CB as radius.

Draw the arc with D as center and DA as radius.

These two arcs intersect at E.

AEB is a blunt arch.

Note: calculation shows that (AE + EB) / AB = Φ, approximately.

FIG. 6-08 ~ Blunt arch adapted to a square plane

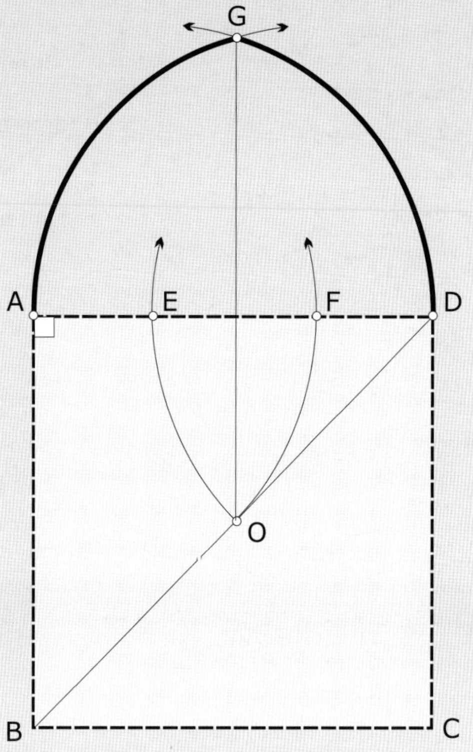

Consider the fundamental square whose side determines the span of arch AD.

O is the center of the square.

Draw the arc with D as center and DO as radius intersecting AD at E.

Draw the arc with A as center and AO as radius intersecting AD at F.

Draw the arc with F as center and DO as radius,
then the arc with E as center and DO as radius.

These two arcs intersect at G which is the vertex of the blunt arch AGD.

Notes: - This figure is drawn by using only one opening of compass equal to DO, the half-diagonal of the square.

- Calculation shows that, by one tenth, GE / FE = Φ and (AG + GD) / AD = Φ thus, the EGF triangle of figure 4-05 page 59 is inscribed in the AGD blunt arch.

FIG. 6-09 ~ Blunt arches drawn by means of a knotted rope

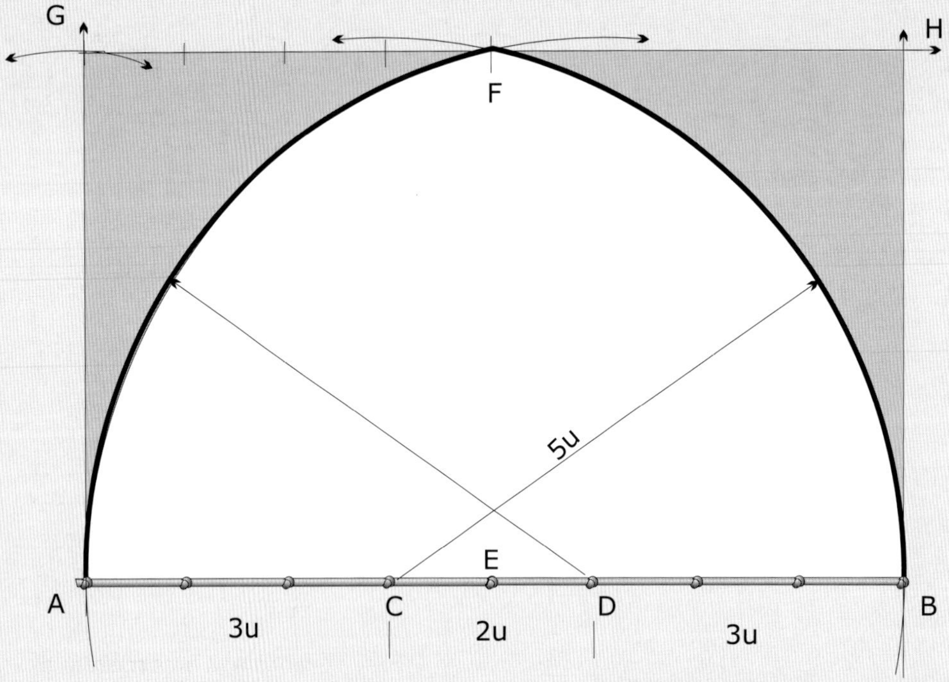

Consider AB = 8u (u stands for a "unit" such as cubit, foot, handbreadth,....)
and E center of AB.

Place points C and D such as AC = 3u and CD = 2u.

Draw an arc with C as center and a radius = 5u.

Draw an arc with D as center and a radius = 5u.

These two arcs intersect at F.

From F, draw the AB parallel intersecting at point G the perpendicular to AB at A.
Similarly you obtain point H.

The AGHB triangle is a golden rectangle.

Notes: - the EF = AG length is slightly inferior to 5u = CF so the ratio AB / AG > 8/5 is closer to Φ than shown in figure 2-13 page 37 (8/5 = 1.6).

- This blunt arch corresponds to those on the tympanums of some cathedrals for example the central tympanum of the Chartres cathedral.

FIG. 6-10 ~ SO CALLED "RAMPANT ARCH", GOLDEN ARCH WITH THREE CENTERS

With the angles of a regular pentagon and decagon

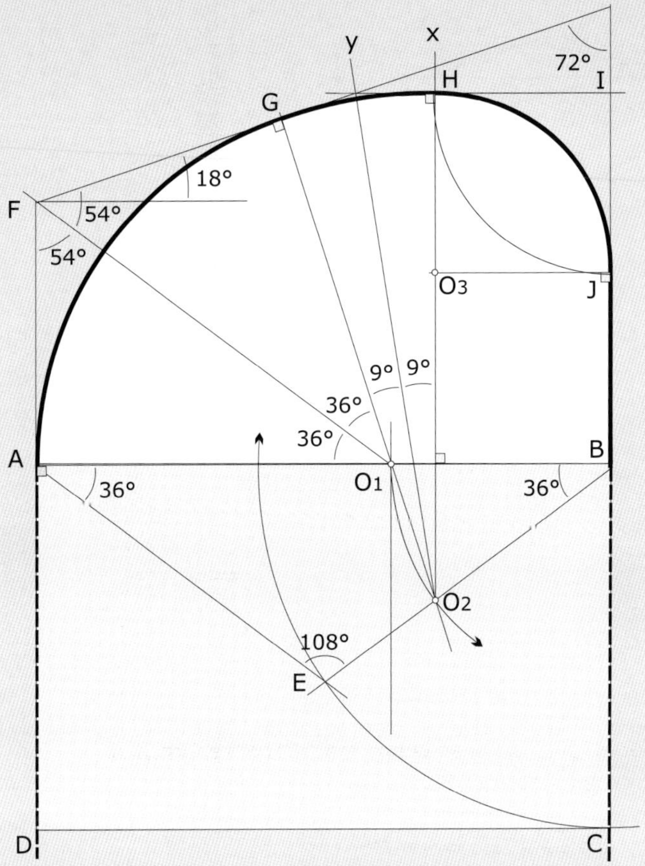

data:
- arch span L = Φ
- rampant angle = 18°
- angles = multiples of 9

conditions to be respected:

see 1-12 page 24

-If an arc is tangent to a straight line, its center is necessarily on the perpendicular to that straight line at the point of tangency.

- when two arcs meet at a same point of tangency, their centers are necessarily on the same axis perpendicular to that tangent: for example, arcs AG and GH at point G.

Draw the golden rectangle ABCD and the isosceles triangle ABE (base = Φ, sides = 1, angles at base = 36°).

O_1 separates line segment AB according to mean and extreme ratio
$AO_1 / O_1B = AB / AO_1 = \Phi$

From O_1 draw the parallel to EA intersecting AD at F.
The symmetrical point to A when considering O_1F is G.
Draw the arc with O_1 as center and O_1A as radius from A to G.

Draw the arc with B as center and BO_1 as radius intersecting EB at O_2.
From O_2 trace the Ox perpendicular to AB, then the bisector O_2y of angle GO_2x
The symmetrical point to G when considering O_2y is point H.

Draw the rampant arch GH with O_2 as center and O_2G as radius.
From H drop the perpendicular to BC intersecting B at I.
On HI build square $HIJO_3$.

Draw the rampant arch HJ with O_3 as center and O_3H as radius.
Thus the rampant arch AGHJ comes into existence with its three centers O_1, O_2 , O_3.

Note: $BO_2 / O_2E = \Phi$ and BI (height of the vault) is quite close to 1.

FIG. 6 11 ~ THE GARDENER'S GOLDEN ELLIPSE

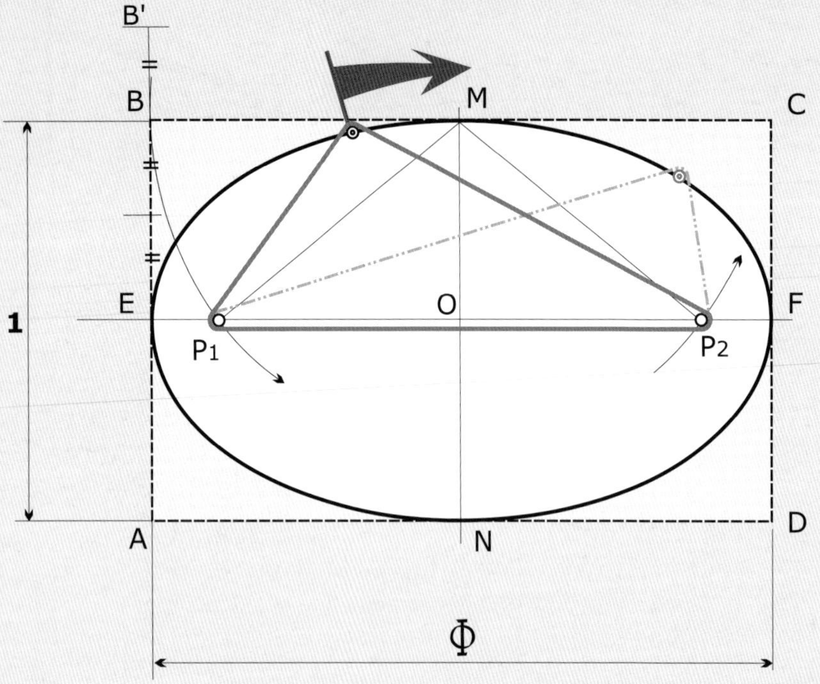

If AB = 1:
the distance (d)
between stakes P_1 P_2
d = 1.27 ≈ **1.25** = AB'

the length of the rope (L)
L = Φ + 1.27 = 2.88 ≈ **3**
or AD + AB′

Drawing the ellipse with a rope to make, for example,
a flower bed according to the golden section.

It must be as simple as possible to make,
the result is estimated by sight so its precision is quite approximate.

The size of the flower bed depends on the **length of the rope**, and according to that length, the **distance between the stakes** will bring about the relationship to the golden section, creating harmony.

Draw the place of the flower bed with a golden rectangle drawn on the ground according to the indications given page 37, fig. 2-15, or more simply by counting steps or with a knotted rope or a decameter, respecting the following conditions:

$$\textbf{length / width ratio} = \frac{AD}{AB} = \frac{\Phi}{1} = \frac{1.618}{1} \approx \frac{16}{10} = \boxed{\frac{\mathbf{8}}{\mathbf{5}}}$$

approximately, the number of knots, of steps or of meters has an **8 to 5 ratio.**

The figure above shows that $Mp_1 = MB$ so $P_1M + MP_2 = BC = \Phi$
hence, the length of the rope: $L = \Phi + P_1P_2$
$P_1P_2 = 2 \times P_1O$ and in the triangle MOP_1 we find $OP_1 = \sqrt{\Phi} / 2$.

So, the distance between the stakes is equal to $\sqrt{\Phi} = 1.272 \approx 10/8$ or rather **5/4 of AB.**

The figure shows this length in AB'.

FIG. 6-12 ~ THE " GEODE " OF THE "CITY OF SCIENCE " IN PARIS

a Take the icosahedron in its circumscribed sphere putting both vertexes on the vertical axis. (5-06, f).

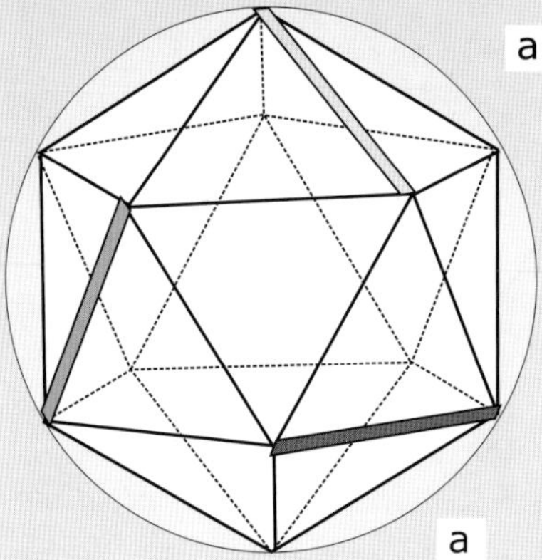

a

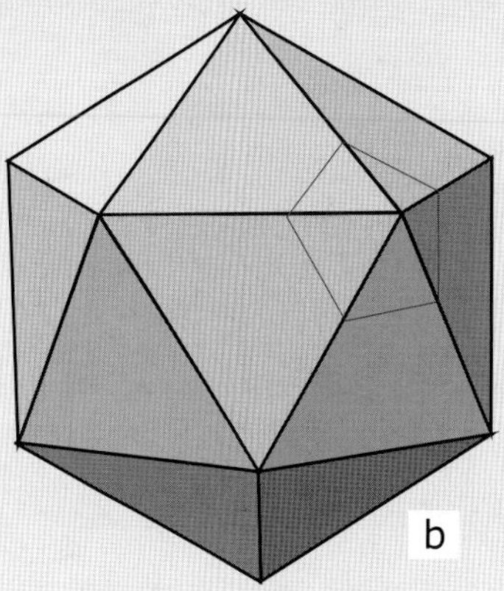

b Isolate the icosahedron and, from one of the vertexes, draw a pentagon that is parallel to the base of the pentagonal pyramid (5-07, c) so as to obtain a point of reference and show the 5 edges starting from that vertex.
Suppose the surface of the solid is elastic and stuck by 12 points at the 12 vertexes.

b

c If you inflate that solid to obtain the circumscribed sphere, without any of the vertex points becoming unstuck, you will obtain the shape of the "geode" with its 20 triangular faces (rounded).
Each face is divided into 100 smaller triangles such as the one darkened in the figure below.

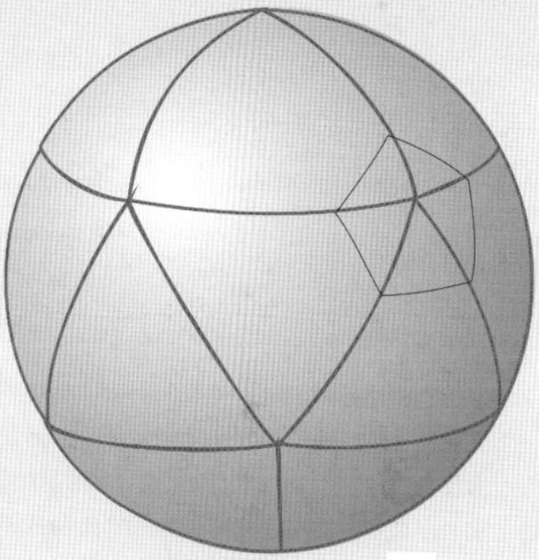

c

d The "geode", imagined and drawn by Adrien Fainsilber and built in 1985 by Gérard Chamayou (French architect and engineer), has only 1670 triangles because the base of the sphere has been cut.

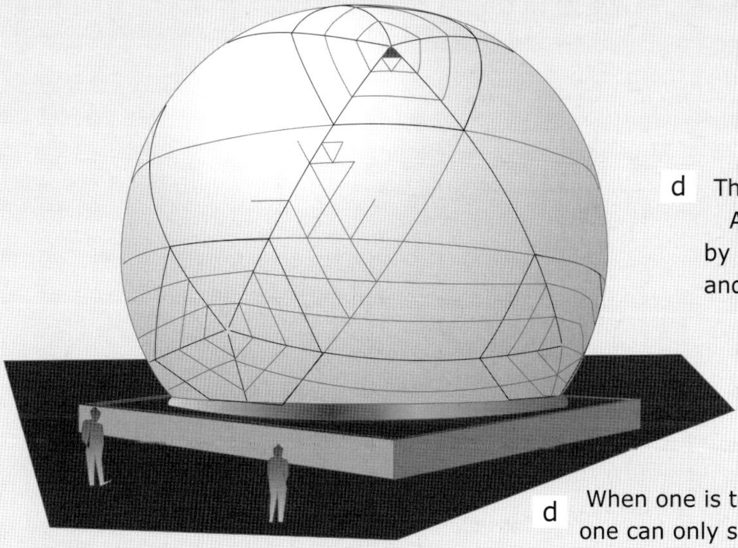

d When one is too near this immense ball one can only see three of its "vertexes".

Fig. 6-13 – a football (soccer) and football grounds

Official football of the International Football Association (soccer). Its geometric construction is identical to that of the "Géode" (6-12 d page 95).

In spite of their various decorations, "on the field" these balls always show their structure composed of pentagonal "vertexes" surrounded by 5 hexagons whose equilateral triangles are variously set off.

The football fields:

It is interesting to note sports grounds are practically all close to the divine proportion in their length-width ratio. This fact would prove the golden section also has a functional aspect!

Football (soccer): Up to 1999 the dimensions where given with a margin that was left to the builders' convenience. The usual dimensions were 105 m by 65 m which gives a ratio of K =105 / 65 = 1.615 $\approx \Phi$
In 1999 it was decided the field would be 105 x 68 hence K = 105 / 68 = 1.544 which increases the width by 3 meters (i.e. 45 thousandth).

Note that the keeper's goal is 7.32 m large by 2.44 m high which corresponds to a rectangle composed of 4 triangles 3-4-5.

4
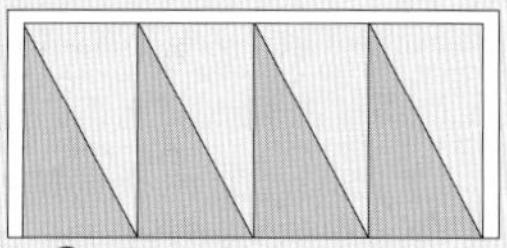
3

Handball: The ground is 40 x 20 m. It is a long square (Barlong square) The goal is 3 x 2 m, it is a rectangle composed of 2 triangles 3-4-5.

Volley-ball: The ground is 24 x 15 m, hence K = 24 / 15 = 8 / 5 $\approx \Phi$.

Rugby: The field is a Barlong square and the ratio between the area of the transversal posts is K = 100 / 68.57 = 1.46

Jai Alai (Basque Pelota): The wall is 16 m large, and 10 m maximum high The ratio is K = 16 / 10 = 8 / 5 $\approx \Phi$.

Bowls: Length = 27.50 m, maximum width 4 m, K = 6.8534 which is exactly Φ^4.
With the minimum width, 2.5 m, the ratio is K = 11, i.e Φ^5 (1 hundredth close)
the ratio between mini and maxi is 4 / 2.5 = 8 / 5 $\approx \Phi$.

fig. 6-14 ~ the tarot of marseille

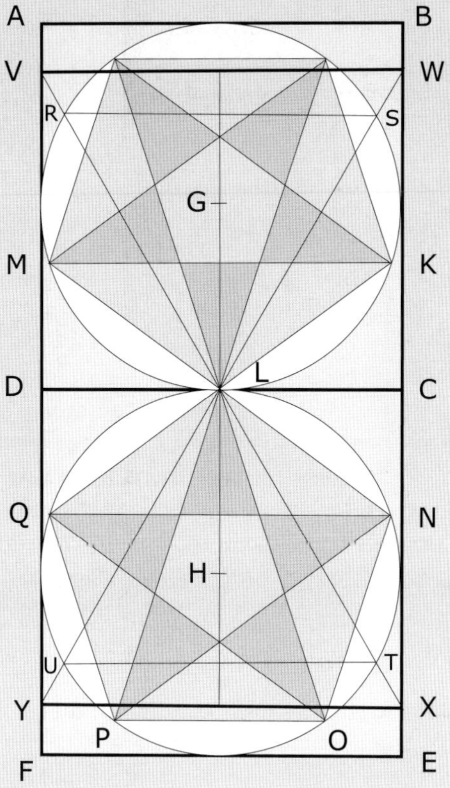

a

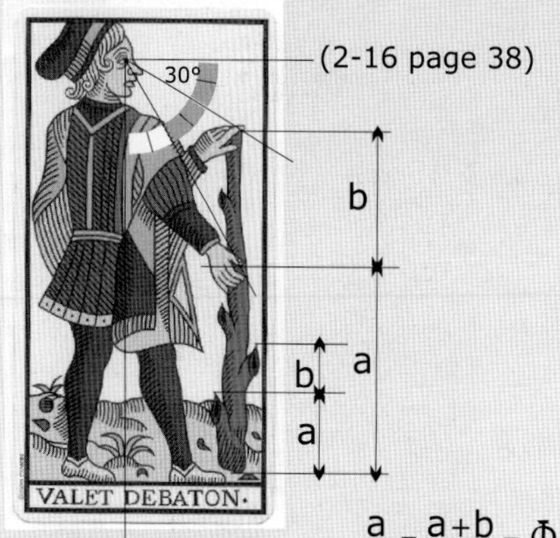

b

$\frac{a}{b} = \frac{a+b}{a} = \Phi$

c

a Geometric drawing of the "lames" (face cards) of the game of the "Tarot of Marseille" and of the façade of the Romanesque and Gothic cathedrals.

The game of tarot has existed at least since 1457, date of the first mention of it by Saint Anthony in his "Treaty of Theology".

In 1781, GEBELIN mentions the "Tarot de Marseille" in book 9 of his "Monde primitif" (Primitive world), but it is around 1760 that Nicolas CONVERT created and made the Tarot of Marseille which has since become famous. It was re-printed in 1965 by the CAMOIN firm. A direct descendant of the firm, Philippe CAMOIN has undertaken, with A. JODOROWSKI, the restoration of the tarot. Here is was he tells us about it: "The restoration of the Tarot of Marseille in 1997 consisted in putting the colours, the symbols and the codes missing in order to make it possible again, after several centuries, to read this true book pregnant with a multitude of symbolic messages".

Many games of Tarot and books about them exist now. Some differ more or less from the rules of the old figures, but the great number of publications is in itself a proof of the interest shown by the public.

To be noted: the set of colours chosen on the same face-card a by Michel ALBERT-VANEL (teacher at the ENSAD, Paris) shows the diversity of possible interpretations. In the old Tarots, the relationship to the divine proportion and to the angles it subtends is obvious as shown in figures b and c .

FIG. 6-15 ~ THE GOLDEN SECTION IN JERUSALEM

The Dome of the Rock in Jerusalem is an important work of islamic art and architecture. It is also the oldest, completed in 692.

Detail of the exterior décor (on the right) on the wall of the Dome which Guy Mourlevat tells us about:
"This ensemble, composed of a rectangle $\sqrt{5}$ inside a golden rectangle, was made in mosaic, in a rigourous way... The 6th century Arabs showed there, under a decorative form, a real theorem of geometry".

Consider the golden rectangle ABCD with AB = Φ and AD = 1.

Inside this rectangle, draw the EFGH rectangle such as
EH = FG = 1 - (1/4 x 2)
and HG = EF = Φ - (1/4 x 2).

You have built the silver rectangle EFGH: the ratio of its sides is $K = \sqrt{5}$.

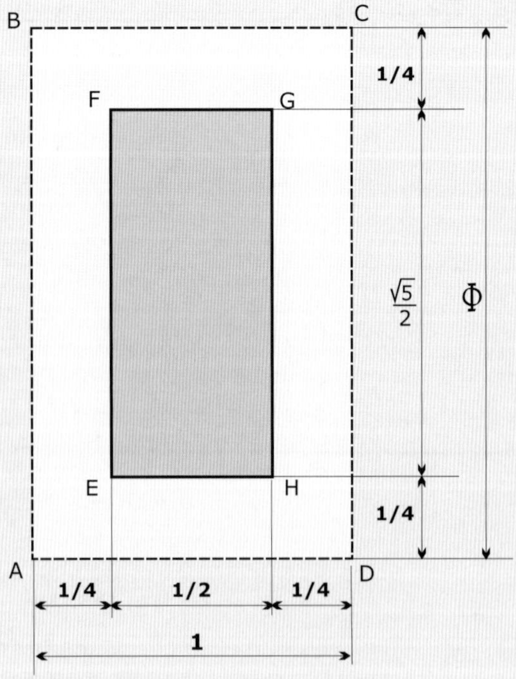

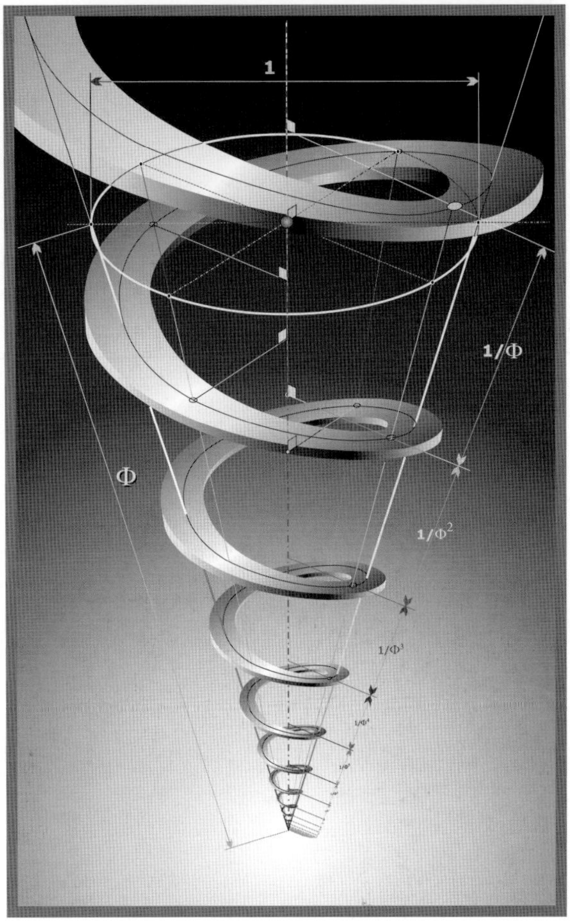

Golden spiral springing from light

Geometrical curios

7

History of the duplication of the cube

Athens is plague-ridden.
The Athenians ask the Delphi oracle how to stop the scourge.
The oracle tells them they must double the volume of their altar which is a cube.
They think they are doing the right thing by doubling the sides.
Thus, they obtain a cube eight times bigger.
The plague continues to decimate the population. The Athenians try another construction.
On the old altar they build a second altar, similar to the first one. Another failure.
Then they build a parallelepiped (not a cube) whose volume is twice that of the cube.
After a lot of research, they build a new cube with AE for side as shown on the construction below.
Their request was then granted.

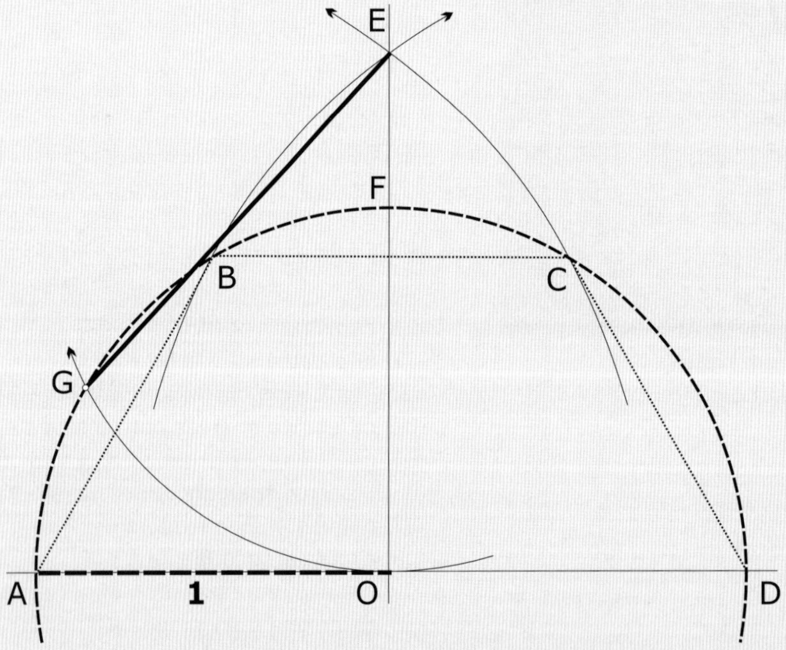

Consider a semi-circle with O as center and OA = 1 as radius.
Draw a regular semi-hexagon ABCD.
Draw an arc with A as center and AC as radius then an arc with D as center and DB as radius.
These two arcs intersect at E.
Consider the middle of arc BC (points E, F and O are on the same line).
Draw an arc with F as center and FO as radius that intersects at G
the semi-circle with O as center and OA as radius.
Line-segment GE = 1.259 = cubic root of 2 with AO = 1.
So GE is the side of the cube whose volume is double that of the cube
with AO as side, equal to the unit.

FIG. 7-02 ~ duplication of the cube with the golden section

approaching drawing

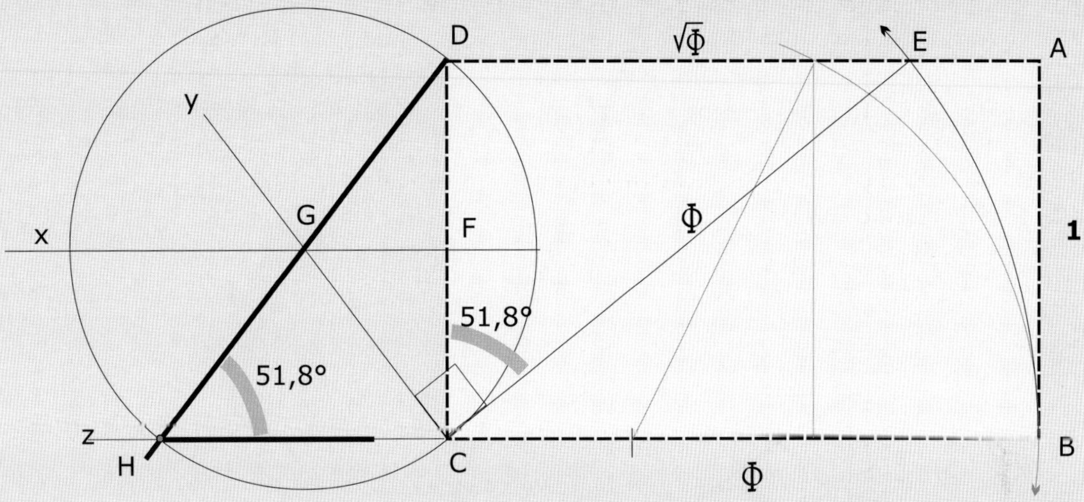

Consider the golden rectangle ABCD.

Draw the arc with C as center and CB as radius that intersects DA at E, CE = Φ, DC = 1, hence ED = $\sqrt{\Phi}$

You obtain the tangent to the angle DCE = $\sqrt{\Phi}$ = 1.272 hence angle DCE = 51.80°

Draw the Fx median of DC.

Draw the Cy perpendicular to EC passing by C that intersects Fx at G (arc 1-06 page 20).

Draw the arc with G as center and GC as radius that intersects Cz (continuation of CB) at H.

The length of the DH line-segment is very close to the cubit root of 2, i.e. 1.260

So DH is the side of the cube which has a volume double that of the cube with DC as side.

Note: the CDE triangle, with its angle = 51.8° is that of the Cheops pyramid (6-03 page 87).

FIG. 7-03 ~ duplication of the cube with triangle 3-4-5

approaching method

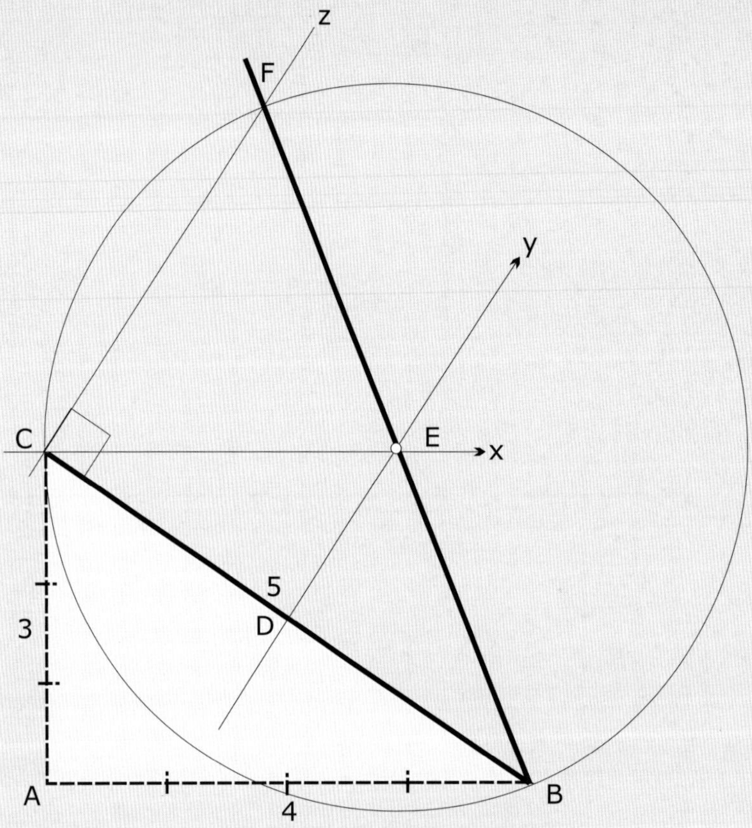

Consider the right triangle 3-4-5, right-angled at A.

Draw Cx parallel to AB.

Draw the median Dy to side BC intersecting Cx at E.

From C, draw Cz perpendicular to CB.

The circle with E as center and EC as radius passes
by points B and C then intersects the continuation of BE at F.

The value of line segment BF is the cubit root of 2 if BC = 1.

So BF is the side of the cube whose volume
is double that of the cube with BC as side.

Fig. 7-04 ~ Difference of area between two regular pentagons, one circumscribed and the other inscribed in the same circle.

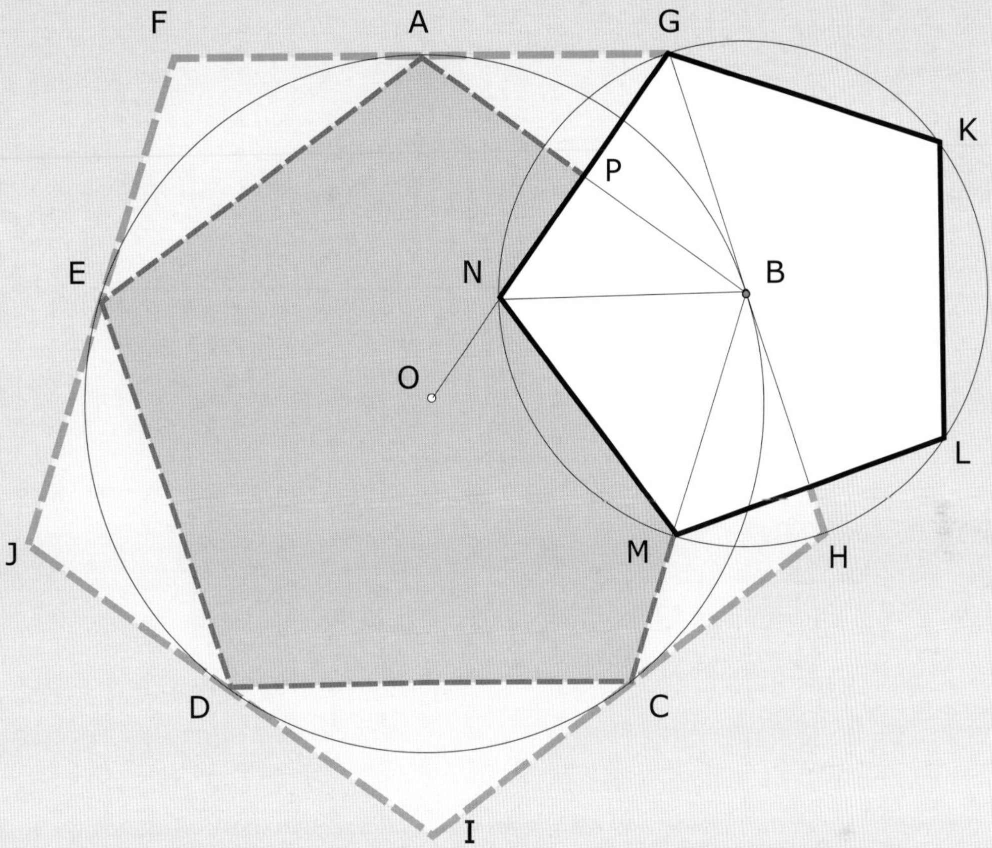

The difference in areas between the regular pentagons FGHIJ and ABCDE
is equal to the area of the regular pentagon GKLMN.

Consider the circle with O as center
and pentagons FGHIJ and ABCDE.

The difference between the areas is equal to five times the isosceles triangle AGB.

The isosceles triangle AGB can be parted into two equal right triangles AGP and BPG.

Consider triangle BPG and draw next to it triangle NPB equal to triangle AGP.

The two isosceles triangles AGB and NGB have the same area.

Note: the area of the regular pentagon GKLMN = 5 times the area of triangle GBN.
It is the difference between the areas of the regular pentagons FGHIJ and ABCDE.

FIG .7-05 ~ PARTING A LINE SEGMENT ACCORDING TO MEAN AND EXTREME RATIO

Drawing Φ and the "quine"

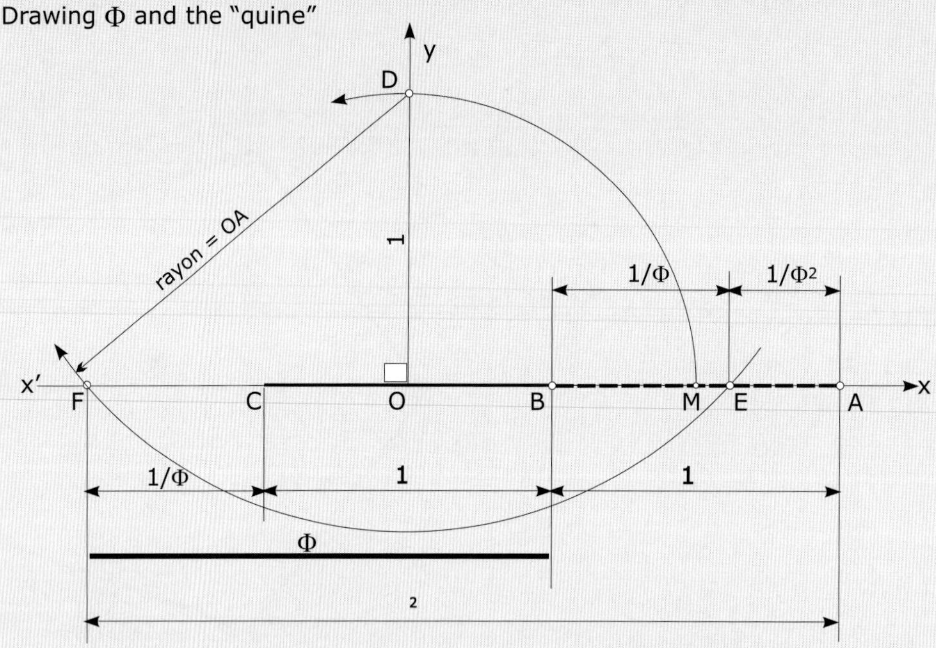

The aim is to part line segment AB according to mean and extreme ratio.

Consider the straight line xx' on which, from A, you situate two equal segments:
AB = BC = 1

Draw O, middle of BC, then, from 0 trace Oy perpendicular to xx'.

Draw an arc with 0 as center and AB = 1 as radius intersecting the straight line Oy at D.

Draw the arc with D as center and OA as radius intersecting xx' at E and F.

You can verify graphically and by calculation that E parts AB according to mean and extreme ratio hence, the ratio: BE / EA = AB / BE = Φ.
Moreover, this figure brings about the following ratios: FB / BA = AF / FB = Φ
or also CB / BE = CE / CB = Φ, or again BC / CF = BF / BC = Φ
with as well, FB / BE = Φ^2 (indeed, Φ / (1/Φ) = Φ^2).

Note: to show the possible modes of mathematical calculations, we give here an example of calculation by analytic geometry (as we did on page 46 by an example of trigonometric calculation).

Equation of the circle with D as center and OA as radius $x^2 + (y - 1)^2 = 9 / 4$
Equation of the xx' straight line: $y = 0$
Intersection between the straight line and the circle: $x^2 + 1 = 9/4$ hence, $x = \pm\sqrt{5} / 2$
abscissa of E = $+\sqrt{5} / 2$, abscissa of F = $-\sqrt{5} / 2$
hence $FA / FB = (3 + \sqrt{5}) / (1 + \sqrt{5}) = \Phi$.

FIG. 7-06 ~ DIVIDING AN ANGLE INTO THREE EQUAL PARTS (TRISECTOR OF AN ANGLE)

approaching method

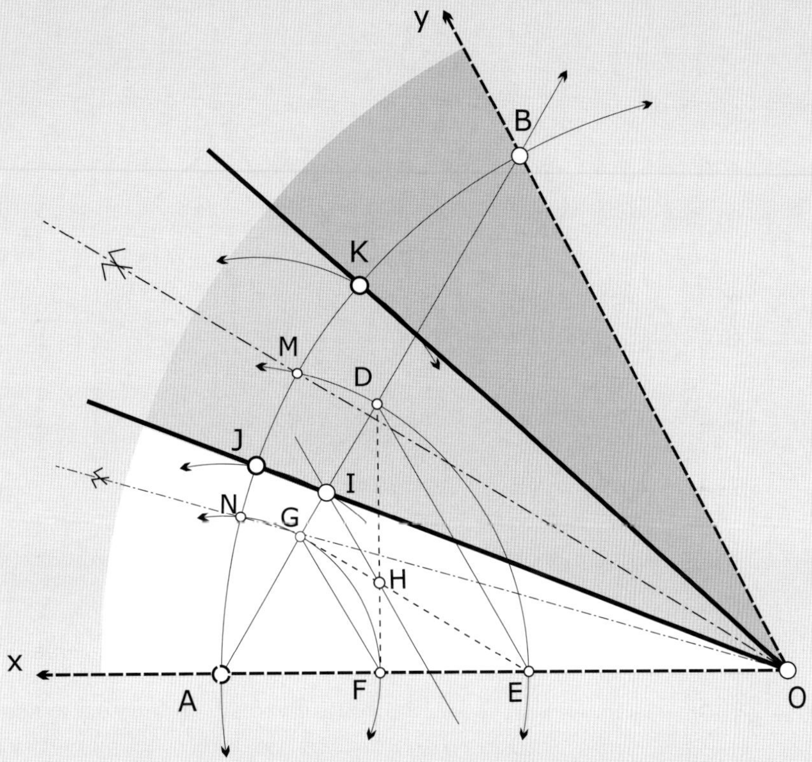

Consider angle xOy and A an unspecified point on Ox

Draw the arc with O as center and OA as radius intersecting Oy' at B: OB = OA
Draw the bisector of xOy intersecting AB at M. The xOM angle is half the xOy angle
Draw the bisector of xOM, intersecting AB at NR. The xON angle is quarter the xOy angle.

For the third of xOy, draw the harmonic mean of the two previous drawings:
- The arc with A as center and AM as radius intersects AB at D and AO at E
- The arc with A as center and AN as radius intersects AB at G and AO at F

from where the GDEF trapezoid whose diagonals GE and DF intersect at H

The parallel to DE passing by H intersects AB at I
The arc with A as center and Ai as radius intersects arc AB at J
From center J transfer the arc with A as radius: it intersects arc AB at K.
(check that KB = AJ)
The OJ and OK straight lines are the trisectors of the xOy angle.

Angles : xOJ = JOK = Koy = angle xOy / 3

Note: The division of an angle into 5 equal parts can be obtained by the harmonic mean between the divisions by 4 and by 6.

FIG. 7-07 ~ BUILDING A REGULAR ENNEAGON [9 SIDES] BY DRAWING THE TRISECTOR OF THE 120° ANGLE

approaching method

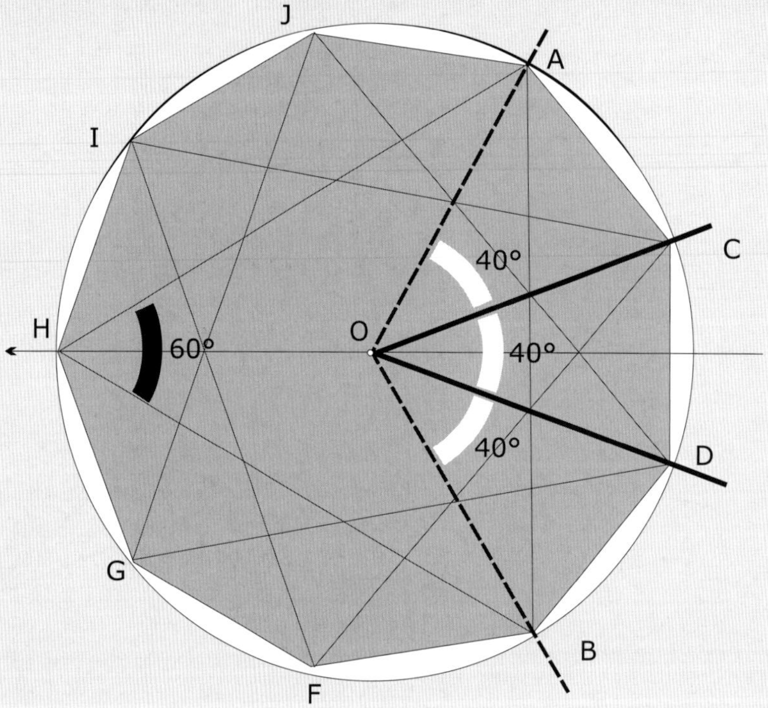

Consider the circle with O as center and R as radius and angle AOB equal to 120°.

Divide angle AOB into three equal parts.

Consider angles AOC, COD and DOB each one of them being equal to 40°.

Draw figure 7-06.

Line segments AC, CD, and DB are the sides of the enneagon.

On the circle with O as center, draw chords BF = FG = GH = HI = IJ = JA = BD

The regular enneagon ACDBFGHIJ has thus been built.

Note: by joining the vertexes three by three, you obtain **three equilateral triangles** ABH, CFI, DGJ. They form a nine ray star.
Angle AHB = 60°, half the AOB angle.

fig. 7-08 ~ circumference, pi (π) and phi (Φ)

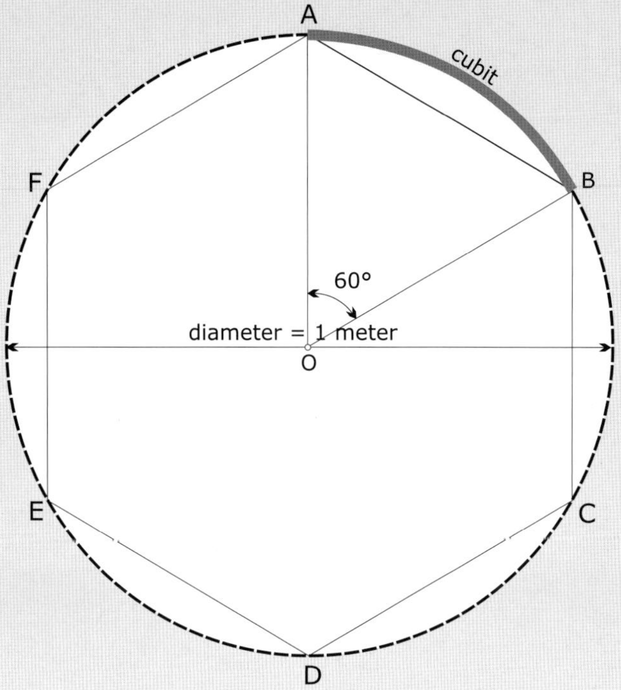

Consider the circle with O as center and a 1 meter diameter.

Draw the inscribed hexagon and the two radii OA and OB forming a 60° angle i.e. one sixth of 360°.

The length of the circumference of the circle is equal to: π x diameter = 3.1416 x 1m.

The length of the arc subtended by chord AB = 1/6 of the length of the circumference (3.1416 x 1) / 6 = 0.5236, which is the length of the royal cubit given in meters

hence: π = 6 cubits / 1 meter.

If the diameter = 0.618 (i.e. 1 / Φ), the length of arc AB will be: (3.1416 x 0.618) / 6 = 0.3236, which is the foot, hence: π = 6 feet / (1/ Φ).

You will also have: π = 6 empans / (1/ Φ^2) = 6 palmes / (1/ Φ^3) = 6 handbreadths / (1/ Φ^4). In the Middle Ages they used one of those measurement units (handbreadth, palme, empan,...) to determine graphically the length of the circumference or of the diameter of a circle.

Note: there are other known ways of expressing π. All are approaching methods (for example π = 22 / 7 = 3.1429). Among them, two will be studied in the next figures (fig. 7-09a, fig. 7-09b) because they give that value according to the **golden number.**

$\pi = 4 / \sqrt{\Phi}$ with $\sqrt{\Phi} = 1.272$ and $\pi = 1.2 \times \Phi^2$ with $\Phi^2 = 2.618$.

fig. 7-09a ~ graphical construction of π

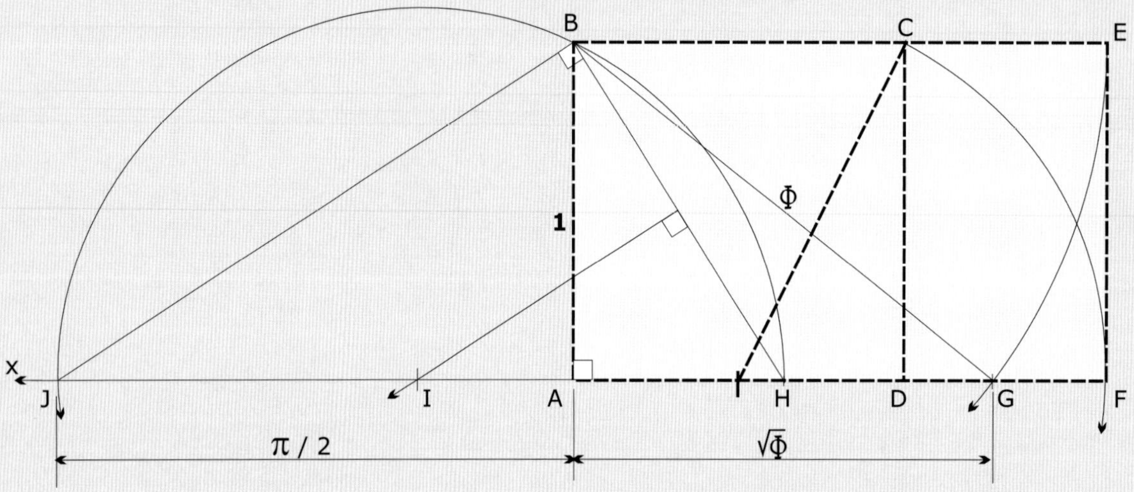

Consider the golden rectangle obtained from the ABCD square, side = 1, AF / AB = Φ.

Draw the arc with B as center and BE as radius that intersects AF at G and BE = BG = Φ.
H is the middle of AG. The median of BH intersects the continuation of AF (Ax) at I
The arc with I as center and IH as radius intersects Ax at J.

You obtain AJ = $2 / \sqrt{\Phi}$, by calculation you know that $4/ \sqrt{\Phi} = 3.1416 = \pi$.

In conclusion, AJ = $\pi / 2$, hence p = $4 / \sqrt{\Phi}$.

FIG. 7-09B ~ GRAPHICAL CONSTRUCTION OF π ACCORDING TO Φ

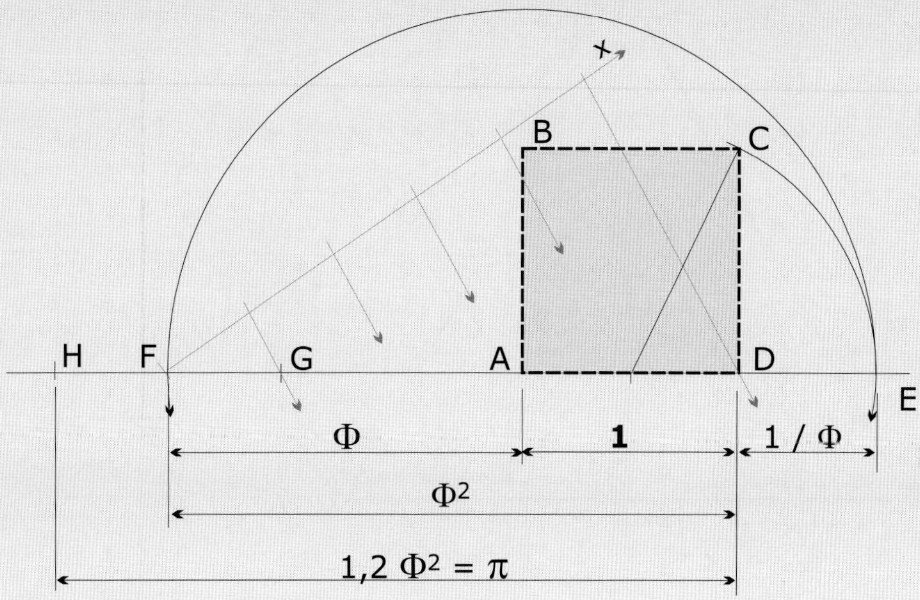

Consider the ABCD square and point E such as AD / DE = AE / AD = Φ.

If you determine AD = 1, you have DE = 1 / Φ and AE = 1 + (1 / Φ) = Φ.

The arc with A as center and AE as radius intersects DA at F
AF = AE = Φ and FA + AD = Φ + 1 = Φ^2.

Divide the FD segment into 5 equal parts by tracing a Fx straight line on which you mark, with the help of a compass, 5 times the same dimension and, from the last point, you join D. The parallels to that last line divide FD into 5 equal parts and FG = FD / 5

Draw on DF, FH = FG, hence HD = 1.2 FD

You obtain DH = 1.2 Φ^2 = π.

Fig. 7-10a ~ Quine and golden spiral with equilateral triangles

from an idea of Mireille Hartmann (Hibon)

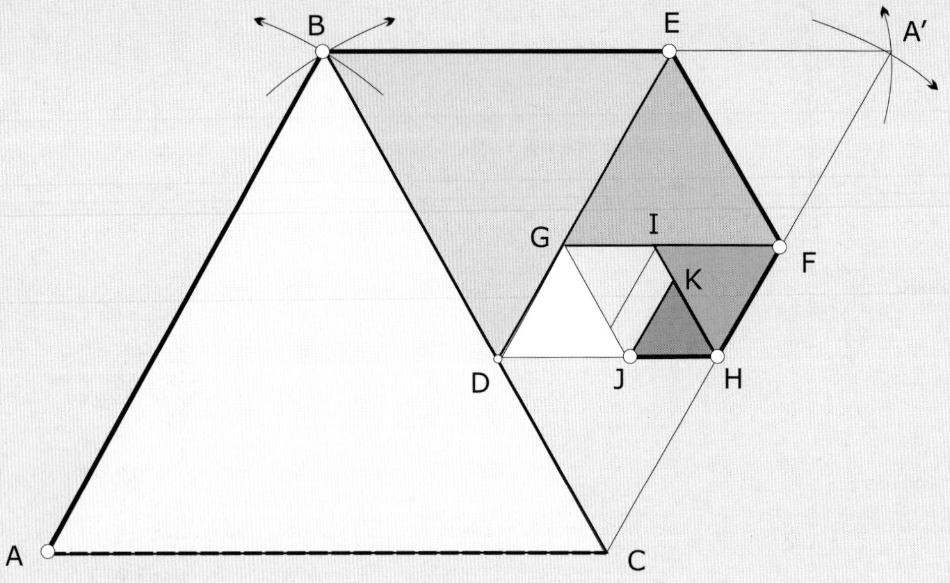

Consider an AC line segment.

From A, then from C, draw an arc with AC as radius to determine B and by consequence the equilateral triangle ABC.

With the same opening of the compass, determine A' from B and C in order to draw another equilateral triangle BCA' so as to make the drawing easier.

On the BC side, determine point D such as BC / BD = BD / DC = Φ.

Thus, D separates BC according to mean and extreme ratio (1-11 page 23). The same will go for points F for DE, I for GF, K for HI, etc.

If AB is the **cubit**, BE will be the **foot**, EG the **empan**, GH the **palme** and HJ **the handbreadth**.

Here again you will find the Fibonacci sequence (page 10):
the elements of the broken line ABEFHJ ...,
show the same characteristics as that sequence:

— any segment = the sum of its two predecessors.
— two consecutive segments have a Φ ratio.

fig. 7-10b ~ golden spiral with equilateral triangles

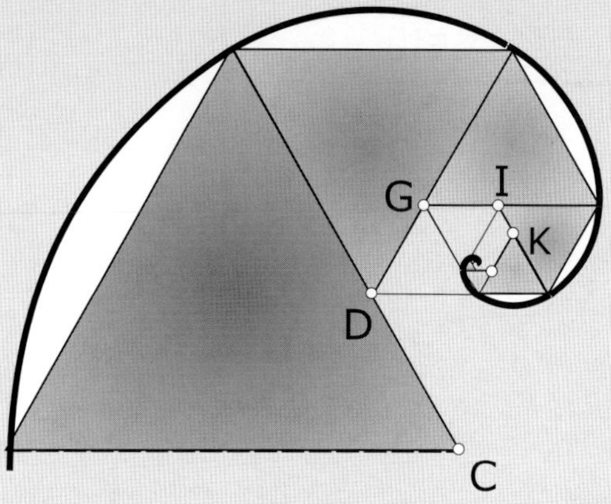

Starting from the previous figure, it is easy to draw the golden spiral, indicating the centers C, D, G, I, K,.... of the arcs constituting the spiral.

Once more, you will notice the two centers on the same straight line to ensure the necessary condition of tangency (1-12 page 24).

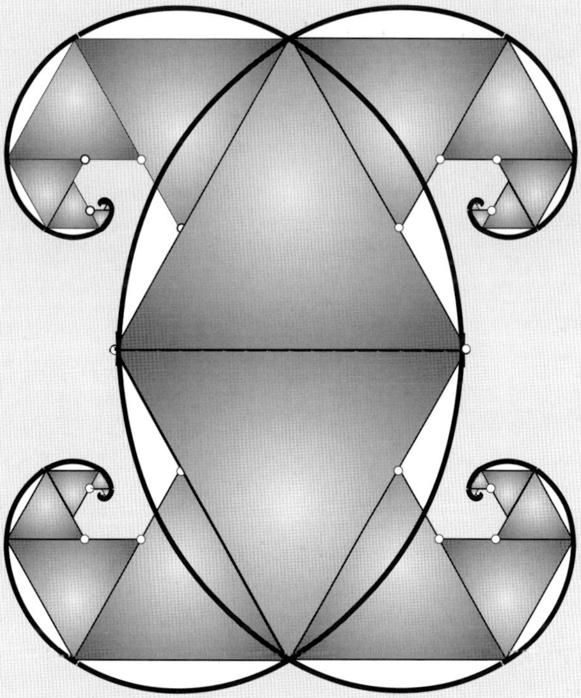

By symmetry or assemblage, it is easy to draw numerous and beautiful figures.

Fig. 7-11 ~ Drawing a regular heptagon starting from an equilateral triangle

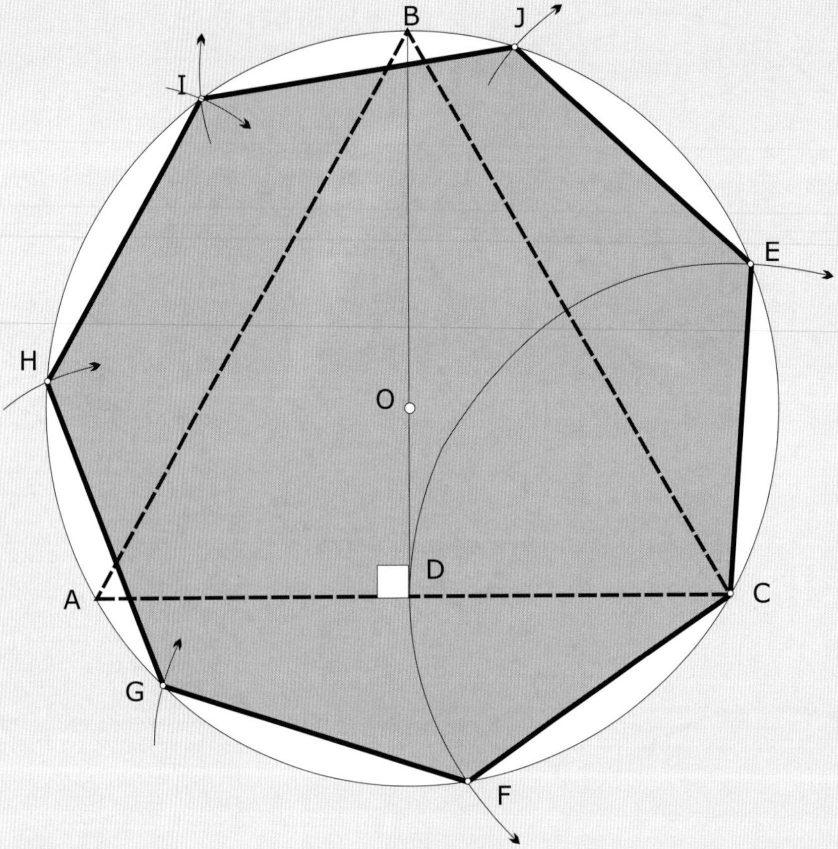

Consider the ABC equilateral triangle with side = 2a, D being the center of the AC side.

The circle circumscribing triangle ABC is also the circle circumscribing the heptagon.

Draw the arc with C as center and DC as radius that intersects the circle with O as center at F and E.
CD = CF = CE, sides of the heptagon with "a" for measure.

Starting from F and E, draw along the circle with O as center
chords FG = GH = HI = IJ = JE = EC = CF = a
(check, for example at I, that the lines coming
from H and J intersect with sufficient precision).

The regular heptagon has thus been built.

FIG. 7-12 ~ REGULAR HEPTAGON BUILT WITH TRIANGLE 4-4-5

with a knotted rope on the ground or with ruler and compass on a piece of paper.

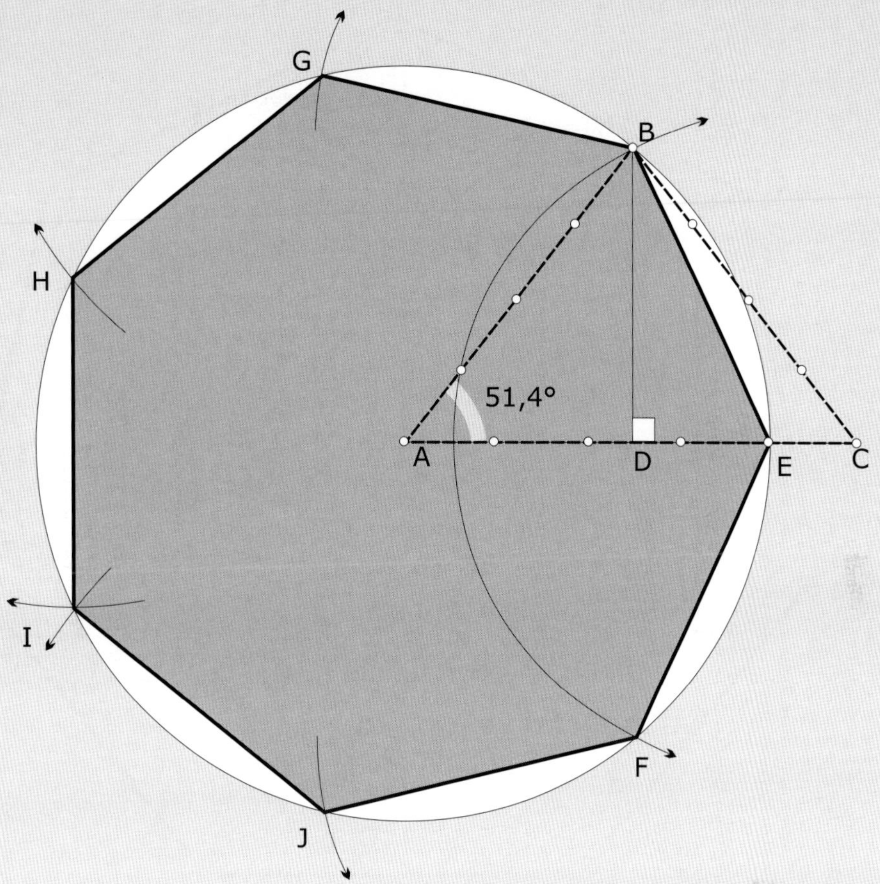

Consider the isosceles triangle (4-4-5) ABC with AC = 5 cubits and AB = BC = 4 cubits.

Draw the circle with A as center and AE = AB = 4 cubits as radius.

This circle inscribes the heptagon.

BE is the side of the regular heptagon BGHIJFE.

Angle BAC = 51.4° (cos = 2.5/4 = 0.625) i.e. approximately the seventh of 360° (360° / 7 = 51.428°).

Triangle 4-4-5 is very easy to draw as one only needs to draw an AC segment of 5 cubits (or feet, empans, steps, ...) and, from the extremities A then C, draw two arcs of 4 cubits intersecting at B.

Note: Constructing the heptagon is mathematically impossible.
Thanks to this very easy drawing it can be made with satisfying approximation.

fig. 7-13 ~ drawing a convex, star-shaped heptagon

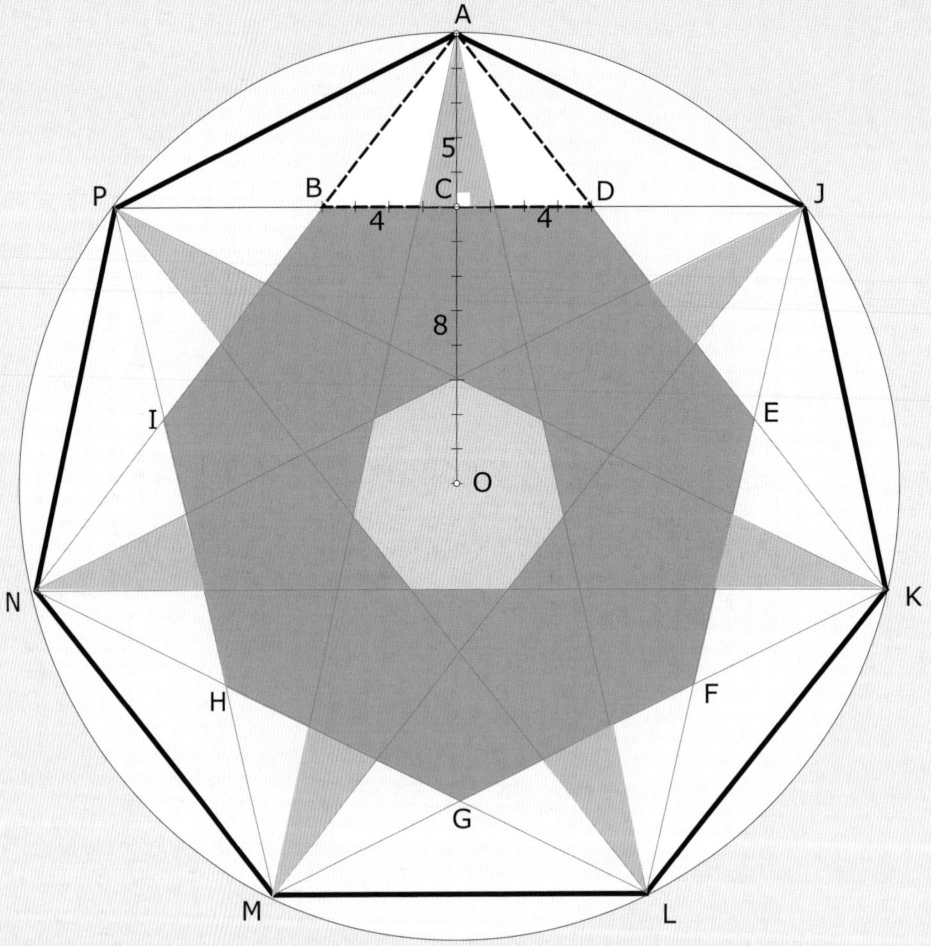

Draw an ADB isosceles triangle with a height = 5 and a base = 8.

On the continuation of the AC median place CO = 8.

O is the center of the circle circumscribing the heptagon (center O, radius OA).

The continuation of segment BD intersects cercle 0 at points P and J.
AP = AJ, sides of the heptagon.

On circle O, trace chords AP = PN = NM = ML = LK = KJ = JA.

The AJKLNMP heptagon has thus been built.

By joining each vertex to all the others, you obtain a
seven-ray star and the two heptagons (in gray).

fig. 7-14 ~ drawing a regular dodecagon with a regular heptagon

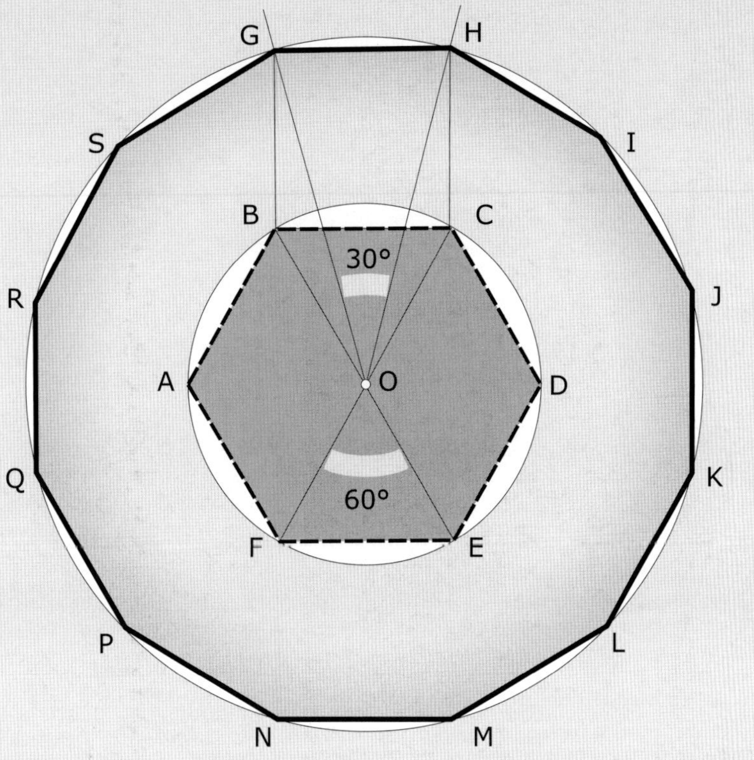

Consider the regular hexagon ABCDEF and O the center of the circle circumscribing the hexagon.

Build square BGHC, with BC as side, on the exterior of the hexagon.
By noting that angle BOC = 60°, and that angle GBO = 150°,
it can be deduced angle BOG is equal to angle HOC = 15°.

So angle GOH = 30° i.e. 360° / 12 (angle at the center of the regular dodecagon)
GH is the side of the regular dodecagon.

On the circle with O as center and OG as radius, trace chord GH twelve times.

You obtain the regular dodecagon GHIJKLMNPQRS.

Note: the 6 squares that could be built on the sides of the hexagon form a rosace
which can be admired in the temple of Diane in Nîmes (France).

FIG. 7-15 ~ DRAWING A REGULAR DECAGON

by a simple and precise method on squared paper with ruler and compass

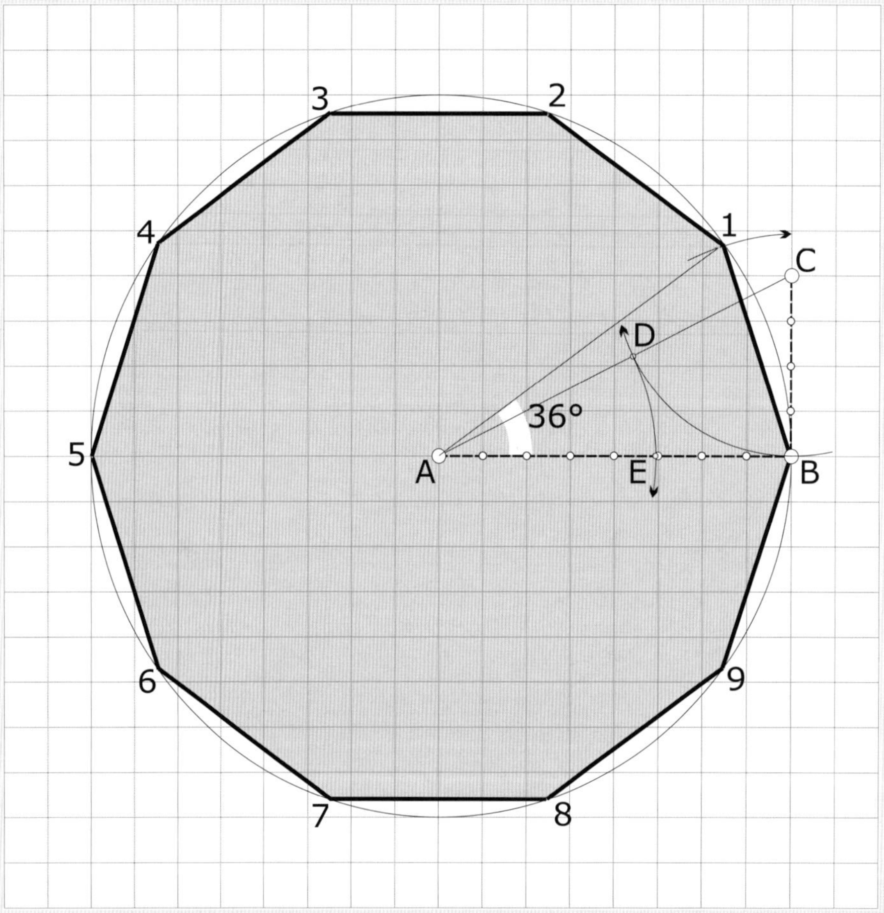

Consider two line segments AB = 8 squares and BC = 4 squares.
Join AC to obtain the half L-shaped square ABC.

Divide AB according to mean and extreme ratio (see basic drawing page 23) thus fixing point D then E with AE / EB = AB / AE = Φ

AE is the side of the decagon inscribed in the circle with A as center and AB as radius.

Indeed, in triangle Ab1, base B1 = AE and side A1 = AB
Hence, AB / B1 = Φ, so AB1 is a **sublime triangle** and the angle at the vertex = 36° i.e. 360°/ 10...... The drawing of the figure is precise.

Draw this chord 9 times on the circle with A as center.
You obtain the regular decagon B123456789.

Notes: — The paper used can be ruled by millimeter or by squares 5x5, 10x10 or any other measurement.
— In a regular decagon: the radius (AB) / side (B1) = Φ.

fig. 7-16 ~ perimetric quadrature of the circle

approaching method

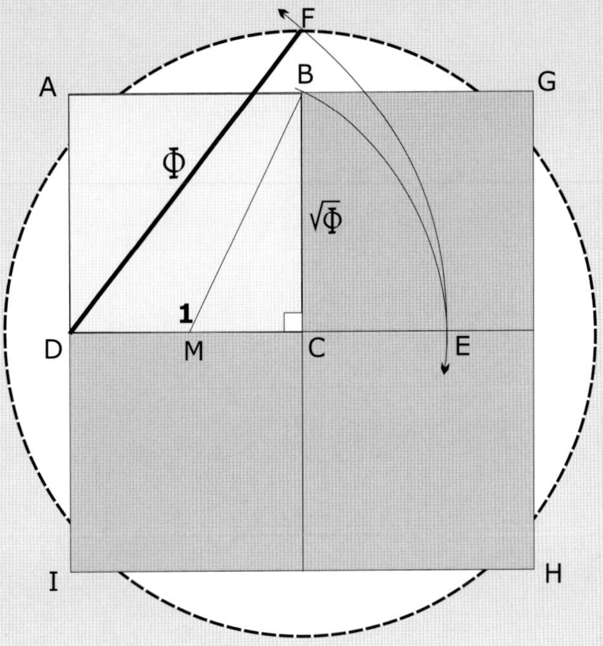

Consider a circle with C as center and FC = $\sqrt{\Phi}$ as radius
Square AGHI, side = 2.

Consider square ABCD, side = 1 and M the middle of DC.

Draw the arc with M as center and MB as radius intersecting DC at E.

Draw the arc with D as center and DE as radius intersecting BC at F.

You obtain triangle DCF such as DF = Φ, FC = $\sqrt{\Phi}$ and DC = 1.

Draw G symmetrical to A considering B, I symmetrical to A considering D and H symmetrical to A considering C.

You obtain square AGHI.

The length of the circumference with C as center and $\sqrt{\Phi}$ as radius is equal to $2\,\pi \times \sqrt{\Phi} = 7.99$

The perimeter of square AGHI is 4 x 2 = 8.

FIG. 7-17 ~ AREOLAR QUADRATURE OF THE CIRCLE

Equality of surfaces between circle and square by means of the Golden Section. Approaching method.

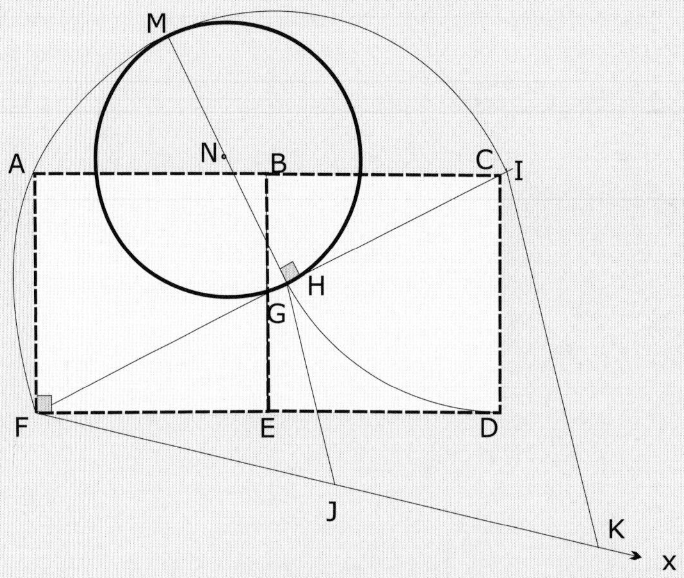

Consider the double square ABCDEF (long silver square).

Draw the half straight line FC intersecting BE at G.

Draw the arc with C as center and CD as radius intersecting FC at H.

Draw an arbitrary Fx straight line and place on it FJ = 6
and JK = 5 of an undetermined unit.
Join HJ.
From K draw the parallel to HJ intersecting FC at I. You will then have HI = 5 / 6 FH.
Drop the perpendicular to FC passing by H.

Draw the semi-circle with FI as diameter that intersects the perpendicular passing by H at point M and draw the circle with HM as diameter.
The ABEF square has the same surface as the circle with HM as diameter.

FIG. 7-18 ~ PERIMETRIC QUADRATURE OF THE CIRCLE

Mercury square by Triangle 3-4-5.

Vitruvius's canon of proportion, made by Leonardo Da Vinci, is the famous drawing of a man inscribed in a circle and a square showing the relationships of his body to the golden section, expressing at the same time the perimetric quadrature of the circle.
The Macrocosmic circle is equal to the microcosmic square.

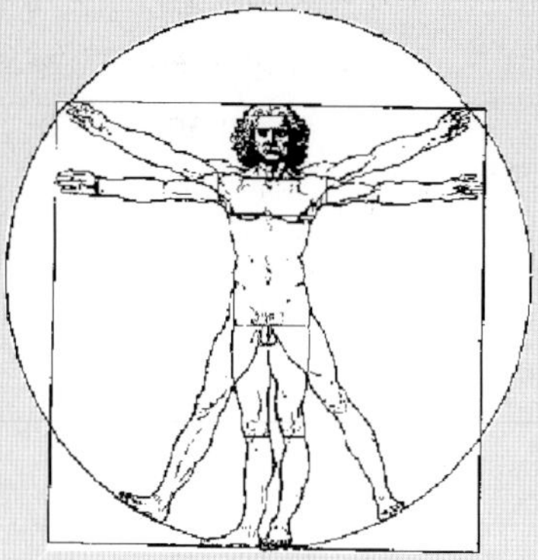

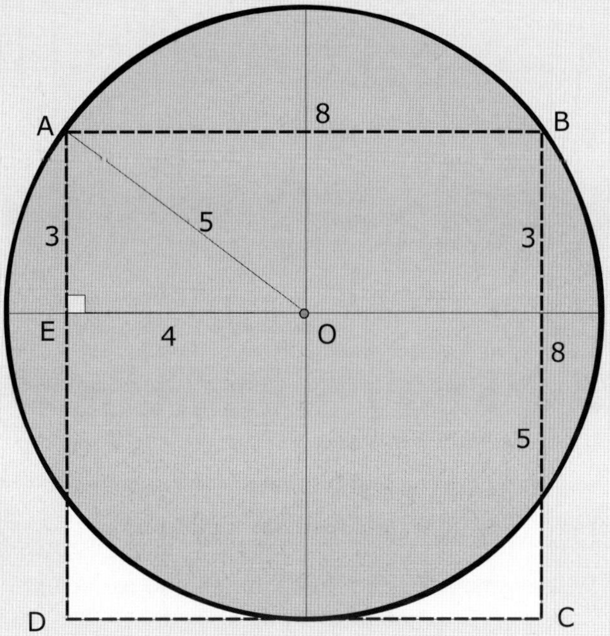

Consider square ABCD, side = 8.

On AD, place segment AE equal to 3 units.

The perpendicular to AD at E intersects the median of AB at point O.
The measure of EO is 4 and AO = 5.

You obtain the familiar triangle OEA (3-4-5), right-angled at E.

Draw the circle with O as center and OA = OB = 5 as radius.

The circle with O as center has the following perimeter
$2 \pi R = 2 \times 3.1416 \times 5 = 31.4$

The perimeter of the square is 4 x 8 = 32.

fig. 7-19 ~ areolar quadrature of the circle

by Triangle 3-4-5.

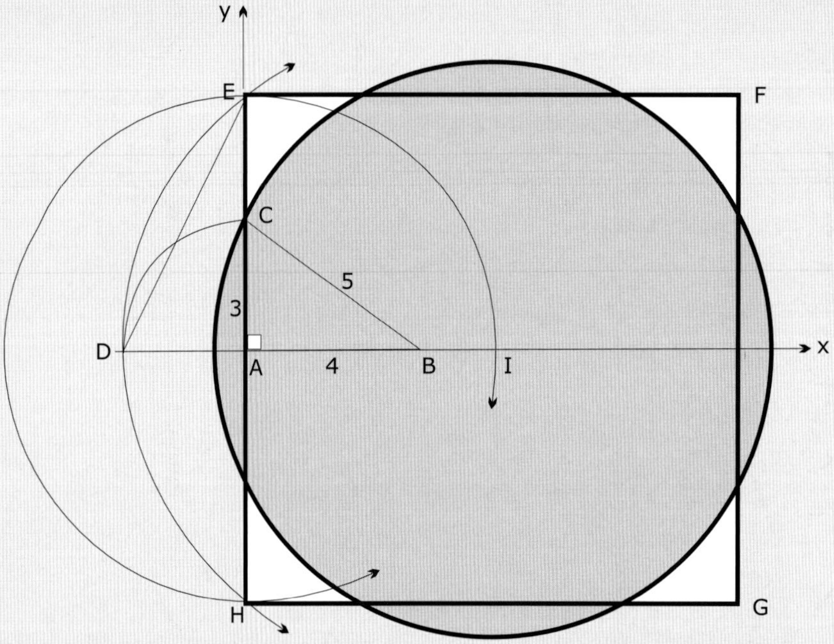

Consider the perpendicular axes Ax and Ay
(obtained by use of the knotted rope: triangle 3-4-5 ABC).

Draw the arc with A as center and AC as radius
intersecting Ax at D.

Draw the arc with B as center and BD as radius
intersecting Ay at E and H.

Draw square EFGH such as AE is the half-side.

Draw the arc with A as center and AE as radius
intersecting Ax at I.

Draw the circle with I as center and IC as radius.

The circle with I as center and IC as radius
has the same surface as square EFGH.

fig. 7-20 ~ equilateral triangle included in a pentagon

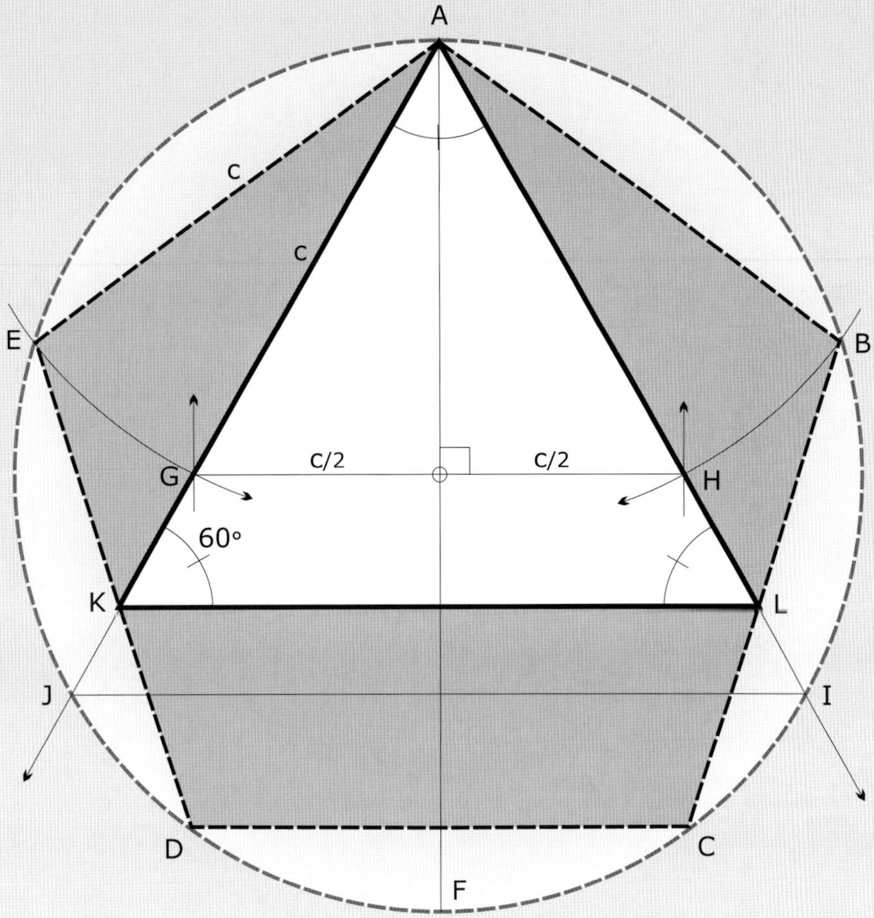

Consider the regular pentagon ABCDE and AF the diameter of the circle circumscribing the pentagon.

Draw the arc with A as center and AE = c as radius then the arc with A as center and AB = c as radius.

Trace the parallels to AF at a distance of c/2 on each side of AF. These parallels intersect the arcs with A as center at G and H.

Triangle AHG is equilateral.

The continuation of AG intersects the circle circumscribing the pentagon at J. The continuation of AH intersects the circle circumscribing the pentagon at I.

You obtain a second equilateral triangle AIJ, AJ intersects ED at K and AI intersects BC at L.

You obtain a third equilateral triangle ALK inscribed in the regular pentagon ABCDE.

FIG. 7-21 ~ REGULAR PENTAGON INSCRIBED IN AN EQUILATERAL TRIANGLE

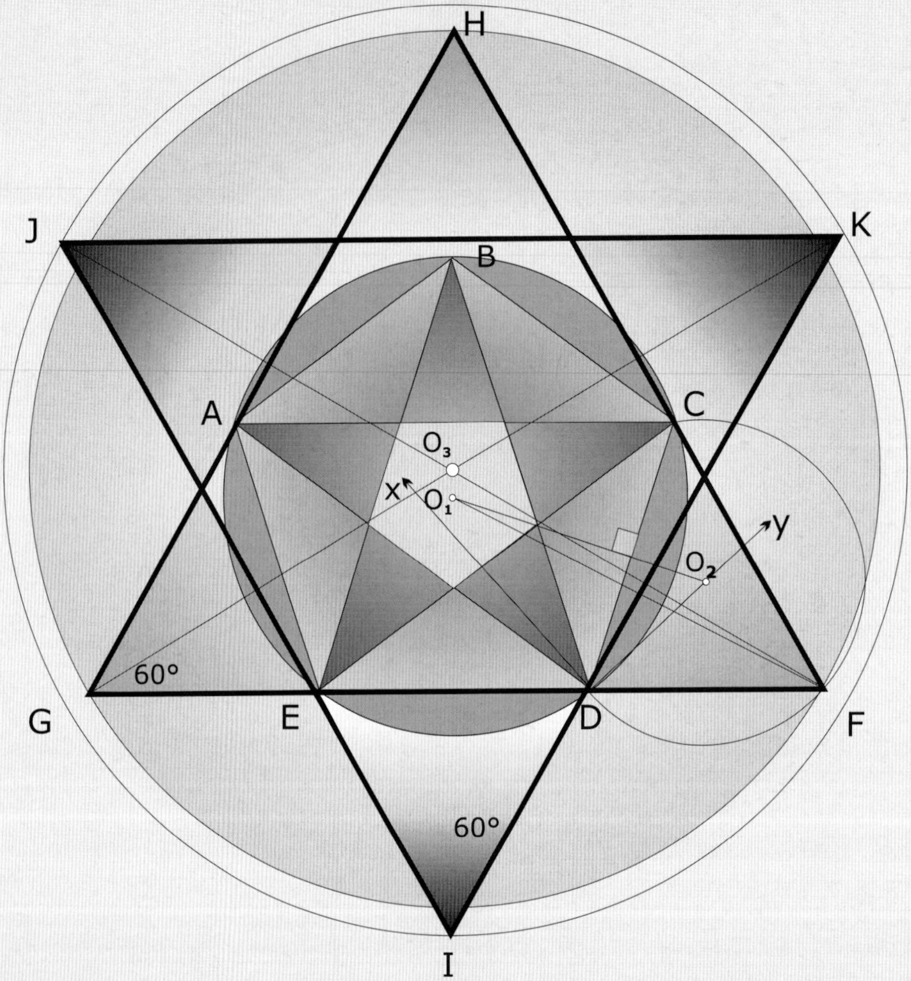

Consider the regular pentagon ABCDE and 01 the center of the circumscribed circle.

To determine F:
Draw the arc of segment DC with an angle of 60° (1-06 page 20).
Consider F the intersection of DE with arc CFD.

On the continuation of DE, place EG = DF.
You obtain the equilateral triangle FGH with GF as side.

Draw the equilateral triangle EDI with ED as side.
The bisector of angle AGE and the continuation of ID intersect at K.
The bisector of angle DFC and the continuation of IE intersect at J.

You obtain the equilateral triangle IJK with 0_3 as center of the circumscribed circle and 0_3I as radius.

0_3 is also the center of the circle circumscribing triangle GHF.

Fig. 7-22 ~ pentagonal star-shaped rosace

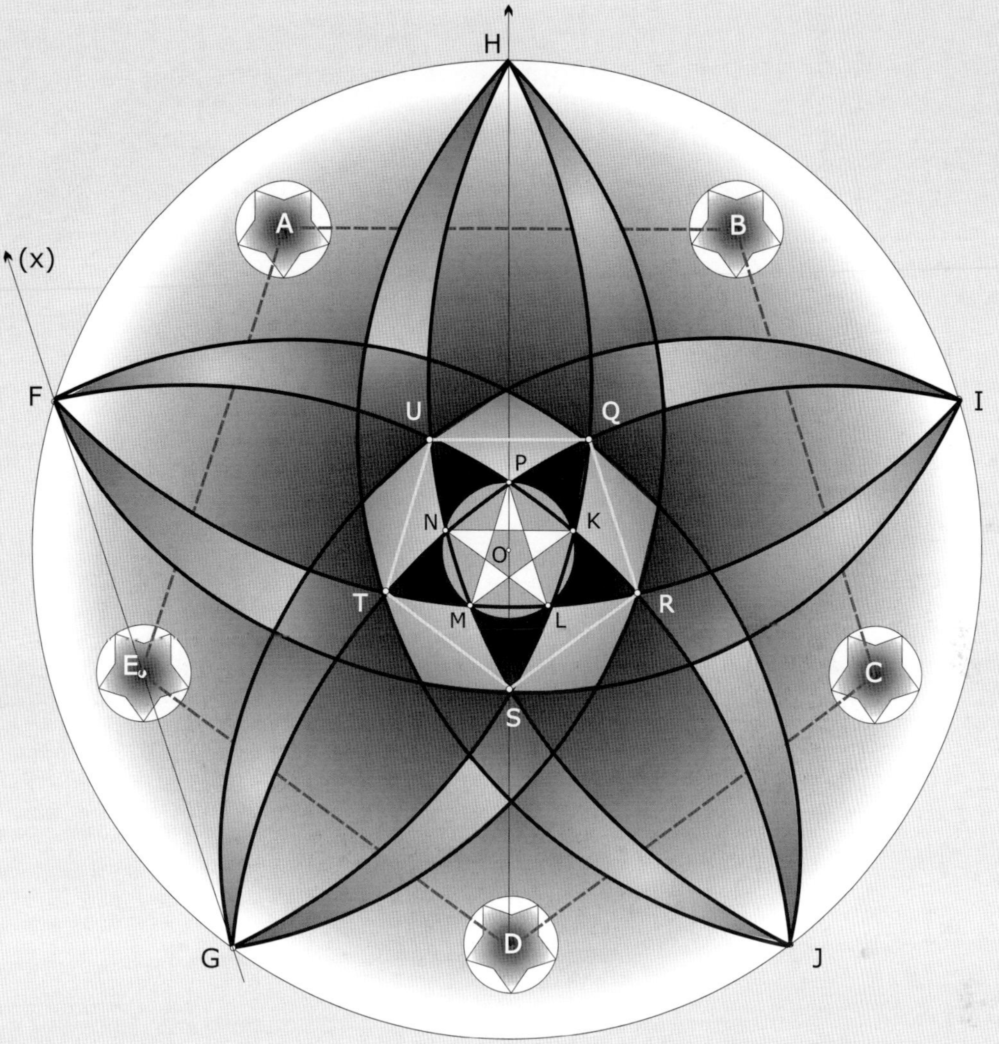

Consider the regular pentagon ABCDE and O the center of the circumscribed circle.

From E, draw the half straight line Ex parallel to BC intersecting straight line CO at F and straight line BO at G. In a similar way, you obtain points H, I and J.

Draw a circle with O as center and with an undetermined radius intersecting EI at K, AJ at L, BG at M, CF at N, and DH at P. You obtain pentagram KLMNP.

Draw arc HG that passes by points K and L (the center being at the intersection of medians HK and GL) and that intersects BG at Q, then draw the arc passing by points L and M and intersecting FC at R. Continue similarly with points S, T, and U.

Thus, you will determine pentagon QRSTU and the star-shaped pentagonal rosace.

what is to be concluded ?

conclusion

"ars sine scientia nihil est"

This is what Jean MIGNOT an architect, asserted around the year 1400.

Indeed, **"art is nothing without knowledge"** and particularly scientific knowledge.
An artist is at the same time an artisan, a technician, a "worker" in the noblest meaning of the word.

This has been fully illustrated by the greatest geniuses since Antiquity, by the builders of our beautiful Romanesque and Gothic constructions, and by the best architects, painters,and engineers throughout times.

We can find true inspiration in their example for our greatest benefit.

Indeed, geometrical constructions contribute to sharpen our faculties for observing and combining, and help to develop a clear and logical mind.

Simplicity, harmony and beauty, are the essence of geometry and in particular the geometry of the golden section which gives us a certain idea of perfection.

It is this perfection that we have wished to exalt and demonstrate in this book.

If we have succeeded in giving the reader the desire to do his own research we shall not have wasted our time nor our enthusiasm.

Reference Books

In addition to the many new figures published here, we have found in each of the following books one or several geometric drawings that can be compared to precious pearls.
I am sure readers will discover a lot of new and exciting figures.

ALLONSIUS *Créer avec un compas*
Édition Dessain et Tolra.-1986-

BAYARD *La Tradition cachée des cathédrales*
Éditions Dangles -1990-

BEGEY *La géométrie sacrée*
Éditions du Rocher 1995
La quadrature du cercle
Éditions du Rocher 1993

BILHEUST *L'art des bâtisseurs romans*
Cahier de Boscodon n° 2-4 et 5 - 1987-88 et 95

CALLANDREAU *Célèbres problèmes mathématiques*
Éditions Albin Michel.-1949

CLEYET-MICHAUD *Le nombre d'or*
Collection – Que sais-je ? – 1973

CROZAT *Système constructif des pyramides*
Librairie du compagnonage

DAVY *Initiation à la symbolique romane*
Collection Flammarion-1977

DECENEUX *Eglises et Cathédrales*
Éditions Ouest-France 1998

FORGET *D'Amon-râ au dodécagone*
Éditions Arma Artis 1983

FOURREY *Curiosités géométriques*
Édition Vuibert et Nony Début du XXe siècle

GALION
Livrets sur Nombre d'Or et polygones réguliers

GIMPEL *Les bâtisseurs des cathédrales*
Édition du Seuil (Collection le temps qui court)

HIBON *L'Enfant et le nombre d'or*
Livret n° 6 Abbaye de Boscodon 1995

HUNTLEY, H.,E., *The divine proportion*
Dover Mathematicals and Science New York 1970

LE MASNE *Le livre des polyèdres* 1988-

LEMONDE *L'ombre du poteau et le Carré de la Terre*
Éditions Dervy 1997

MASCHERONI *La géométrie du compas*
Édition Momom-1798-(1980)

MATILA-GHYKA *Le nombre d'Or*
Édition Gallimard 1959

MOURLEVAT *Le nombre d'or et l'architecture romane en Auvergne* Centre Régional de Documentation Pédagogique. 1980
Géométrie et symbolisme dans une église romane
Notre Dame du Port CLERMONT-FERNAND (1993)

NEROMAN *Le nombre d'Or (Clé du monde vivant)*
Édition Dervy-1981
La leçon de Platon
Éditions Arma Artis 1997

NEVEUX et **HUNTLEY** Le nombre d'or
Éditions du Seuil 1995

NIMOSUS Christiama *Le monde secret des croix*
Guy Trédaniel Éditeur 1990

PACIOLI *Divine proportion*
Librairie du compagnonnage -1988

PEREZ *L'ADN décrypté*
Édition Résurgence Belgique

PERNOUD *Sources et clefs de l'art roman*
Berg Internationl 1980
Pour en finir avec le Moyen-Age
Éditions du Seuil 1977

SARRADE *Sur les connaissances mathématiques des Bâtisseurs des cathédrales*
Librairie du Compagnonnage 1986

ROUBAUDI *Géométrie descriptive*
Masson Éditeur 1935

STUTZ *Esthétique Géométrique*
Modern'Graphic 1995

VINCENOT *Les étoiles de Compostelle*
Éditions Denoël 1982

WALSER *Der Goldene Schnitt* B.G. Teubner, Stuttgart 1996.
Translation from German Edition of Hans WALSER: *The Golden Section* 2001, Published and Distributed by The Mathematical Association of America (USA)

WARUSFEL *Les nombres et leurs mystères*
Édition du Seuil (Point science)

WENZLER *Architecture religieuse romane*
Éditions Ouest-France -1997

INDEX

Pervenche.